JUST A NOBODY

JUST A NOBODY

AN AUTOBIOGRAPHY

"CHANGE A THOUGHT,
MOVE A MUSCLE"

XULON PRESS

Xulon Press
555 Winderley Pl, Suite 225
Maitland, FL 32751
407.339.4217
www.xulonpress.com

© 2024 by Joseph A. Seabolt

All rights reserved solely by the author. The author guarantees all contents are original and do not infringe upon the legal rights of any other person or work. No part of this book may be reproduced in any form without the permission of the author.

Due to the changing nature of the Internet, if there are any web addresses, links, or URLs included in this manuscript, these may have been altered and may no longer be accessible. The views and opinions shared in this book belong solely to the author and do not necessarily reflect those of the publisher. The publisher therefore disclaims responsibility for the views or opinions expressed within the work.

Unless otherwise indicated,Scripture quotations taken from the English Standard Version (ESV). Copyright © 2001 by Crossway, a publishing ministry of Good News Publishers. Used by permission. All rights reserved.

Paperback ISBN-13: 979-8-86850-441-9
eBook ISBN-13: 979-8-86850-442-6

Dedication

This book is dedicated to those who have ears to hear and eyes to see! My hope is that all who read these words see not just the story being told but the One who is truth! He's given me a "tool set" specific to recovery, that He wants me to use to do for the work that it is intended to accomplish. The work He started and will finish on the day of His return.

For those who are like I once was…
Jesus has a plan!

"No temptation has overtaken you except what is common to man, God is faithful, and will not allow let you be tempted beyond your ability, but with the temptation he will also provide the way of escape, that you may be able to endure it." (1 Cor. 10:13 ESV)

A special thank you to Ron Norr, who is my tour guide to Christ, recovery, and accountability. Next to my wife and Jesus, you are my best friend. If there were a mentorship scale, you would be second on the list, with Jesus first and my earthly dad third. Thank you for answering your call to walk out the life Jesus has drawn for you. Never forget what a true miracle you are to and for others. I love you Ron.

To my wife, I love you, who without you answering the call to believe in Jesus, this story would be very different. We move individually where He needs us to be, and He keeps us together to achieve His purposes. Thank you beautiful for always having my back and believing with me!

My daughter Danielle, who is gracious enough to contribute to this work. I don't deserve to be part of your life, and I know to have a relationship like we do, is not the "norm" compared to most stories like mine. Thank you, sweetie, I love you.

Foreword

When I first met Joe, it was at a Celebrate Recovery meeting at our church. He was confronted with a huge, life changing experience of possibly going to prison for DUI and other crimes. I was impressed with his composure. He was concerned but strong in his fortitude, even though he was a rookie in his Christian faith.

Joe Seabolt is like a love magnet. When you meet him, you know he cares and is listening. He is one of the first people you would call when facing troubling issues in life.

He always has a deep insight to life, and you can't surprise him. When sharing your life with someone, do you really want answers, or someone who cares? Go to God for questions and answers. Go to your friend(s) for companionship in your life walk.

In Joe's autobiography you will find out who's in charge of Joe's life. Hopefully, you will find who's in charge of your life as well. You don't have to be around Joe long before you see it in action. You can feel compassion in his voice. He doesn't have to have the answer to everything, because he is a true friend.

Nelson Simpson

Contents

Dedication. v

Foreword vii

Introduction. xi

Chapter 1: People, Places & Things 1

Chapter 2: Experience 67

Chapter 3: Strength. 98

Chapter 4: Willingness. 102

Chapter 5: Honesty 115

Chapter 6: Provision. 146

Chapter 7: Hope. 167

Introduction

"He saved us, not because of works done by us in righteousness, but according to his own mercy, by the washing of regeneration and renewal of the Holy Spirit, whom He poured out on us richly and through Jesus Christ our Savior, so that being justified by his grace we might become heirs according to the hope of eternal life."
(Titus 3:5-7, ESV)

We all have mountains in our lives… mine is the ability to love people. I don't "love" people; I'm always looking "at" people, judging them, and sizing them up to see where they fit into this world. I am looking to see what character they have and what their role is in this life. I am always trying to figure out if people are genuine, comparing them to myself and to my heart, when who I truly need to be looking at is Christ. I should be comparing myself to Christ! I should be comparing my heart to His and asking am I being genuine? What is my role in this world? What does He want me to do? Well, I heard to be transparent, completely transparent! That's what I'm going to do here.

I watched Alex Honnold free climb El Capitan on a streaming channel. He was free climbing with no ropes! El Capitan is an actual mountain, but it also represented a "mountain" in Alex's life. Free climbing El Capitan was a goal in Alex's life, and it was also a stumbling block and the greatest, most riveting moment of his life. It was the climb of a lifetime. There is so much to say about what that climb meant to Alex, but only Alex knows!

Thank you, Alex, for being who God made you to be. I was in awe of you as I watched you succeed in climbing El Capitan. I pray that if you do not know this, you will come to know that Jesus made you just the way you are and that this is His plan for your life. The reason you can do what you do is because of Him. I pray that He will give you that knowledge. The fact that you can do this is not only because of your own discipline, painstaking hard work, determination, and years of training, it is a special gift you have been given from Christ. He created your gift in you before the foundations of the world were ever put into motion. You were

Introduction

created for a purpose. I pray you are His. He makes us who we are from the inside out, puts us where He wants, and writes our story before we ever take our first step. In Him we have hope!

Chapter 1
People, Places & Things

*"The heart of man plans his way,
but the Lord establishes his steps"
(Proverbs 16:9 ESV)*

There is a battle going on between the devil and God for my soul. I heard this from the time I was old enough to understand. My mother was the first to talk to me about this. Throughout my life, I have had supernatural experiences, seen some things, heard some things, and learned enough to know the battle is real. I am living proof there is not just a battle going on… it's an outright war!!!

On October 28, 2012, my ex-girlfriend called me sometime late in the morning, not knowing that I had been up since the night before hung over. I was still coming down from smoking crack earlier that morning when I was trying to help my friend, Tammy, with some work on her van. Not mechanic work but interior "pimp my ride"-type work. I was looking to make some money, of course, to buy more drugs. My ex asked me if I would like to go to Starkey Park for "Halloween Haunted Trails." My daughter, Danielle (D for short), wanted me to go. We went there most years as a family, so I didn't hesitate to say yes because I loved them both. My ex and I weren't together at that time, so any time with them was important, and I wanted to be there for them.

"King alcohol" was going to need to be in charge though, because I was a mess, and alcohol was the only thing that was going to "get me right" or help me be able to act somewhat normal. I needed Tammy to pay me first so I could get some booze. After I got paid, I drove a company truck from Clearwater, Florida, where I was living off Fort Harrison Road, then to my ex's house in Holiday, FL which was about a forty-five-minute drive with traffic. When I got to her house, I realized I had forgotten to stop at the liquor store. I had already finished one pint on the drive there, and I needed more to take with me. I asked my ex what time we were leaving, and she said, "You got ten minutes." So, I decided to take a ride to the liquor store.

My daughter Danielle and her friend, our so-called adopted daughter, Chipmunk, one of Danielle's closest friends, wanted to come with me to get some chips. I said yes but told them they could not ride in the bed of the truck. "You got to get in the cab," I said, "so I don't get pulled over." Well, when we got to the liquor store, they didn't have the chips the girls wanted, so we went down the street to the Kangaroo Mini Mart to get them. When we came out of the store, the girls jumped into the bed of my truck where there were steel pipe fittings in buckets, a pipe threading machine, a windboard strapped to the rack, and some other stuff that could possibly hurt them. For some reason all of that didn't matter at that time. I just thought, *we aren't far from the house. I'll give them a thrill ride!!* I gunned it off the line at the light and headed down Grand Boulevard South toward the house. It was a twenty-five-mile-per-hour zone, and I got up to eighty-five miles per hour before I got to the "S" bend.

My daughter was twelve and Chipmunk was a teenager, and I was driving drunk while on a revoked/suspended license. My license had been suspended since 2006. I was speeding, drunk, hung over, and endangering the lives of my children, and everyone else for that matter. Just take a moment to let that all sink in. Anything could have happened, and this story may have been very different, but here's what happened.

In the eight seconds it may have taken me to get from zero to eighty-five, I watched my daughter smile, stand up in the bed, and then quickly start to crouch down behind the tailgate as if to hide from something. While watching her in the rear-view mirror, and in the near distance, I could see the red, blue, and white bubble gum machines (police lights) going off behind me. Then I heard the sirens. I took my hand, put it out the window, and commenced to wave the cop around the truck, and started to slow down. *Go get em' officer*, I was thinking. Yeah, I didn't get it… until I did… then it hit me so quickly. The information started to come through my tiny little brain, like a download on a computer.

- My daughter was hiding to protect me from getting pulled over.
- I was drunk and speeding with them in the bed of the truck.
- I have no license.
- He's pulling me over!
- I could have killed them!

I started to shake because I was scared. The other thing that was going on was this. I told you I saw my daughter try to hide herself. She was trying to hide from the police so they wouldn't notice her and pull me over. She was trying to help me. Well, what was I doing to help keep her? Keep her safe and show her that I loved her?! You guessed it, nothing. I was doing just the opposite of what a loving father should have been doing, protecting his child from harm. I *was* the harm. As my wife would say, I was dangerous.

I was pulled over, and the girls were taken out of the bed of the truck. I was told to sit tight, turn the truck off throw the keys out the window, and stay in the vehicle. Once the officer had the girls safe, he approached the truck and said, "Just tell me you're not drunk." I said, "I'm drunk, officer." He got me out, handcuffed me, and sat me in his cruiser till the DUI officer showed up. While waiting he asked, "Are they your children?" I told him Danielle was mine and the other girl was her friend whom I thought of like my own. He just shook his head and said, "I can't believe any father would do what you were just doing," and he handed me over to the other officer.

He got the girls back home and verbally tongue lashed my ex about what a bad mother she was. There was no accident, no one got hurt, and the police did exactly what they were trained to do and kept everyone safe that night. I was arrested on October 28, 2012, and the company truck was impounded until the company decided if they wanted to press charges or not. What a blessing that they didn't. I was charged with two counts of felony child neglect—my fourth felony driving while license suspended with knowledge, my third felony DUI within ten years (should have been fourth), and a felony habitual traffic offender.

After getting to the Pasco County Detention Center (county jail), being booked, and going through the process once again, I was brought into the population. I was placed in Charlie Wing, C100, just three days before Halloween. I couldn't have felt more useless, worthless, and hopeless than at that point. The shame of who I had become, and all the things I had done to people I loved and others throughout my life, was weighing on me heavier than I ever felt before. The Hulk could have swung me around like he did with Loki, and it wouldn't have had much of an effect or been punishment enough for me. I could not shake the memories, the feelings, the emotions, the hatred for myself. I did not want to deal with it any longer. All hope was gone. I just wanted it all to stop, for me to stop! Stop abusing drugs, stop wanting drugs, wanted stop lying, stop stealing, stop manipulating, stop drinking, stop hurting people, stop abusing people, stop using people, stop hurting, and just stop living. I wanted to die!

I was convinced I could not change, no one could help, and God was a lie. I would never be the "exception to the rule" talked about in AA. I wasn't going to ask for help, I wasn't going to pray to a "God of my understanding," I wasn't going back to AA, I wasn't going to go to meetings, and I wasn't going to try to figure it out again. I decided to wait until they passed out razors to shave with, and I would use the blade in the razor to slit my throat and bleed out right there in C100. I would finally get all that mess over with and remove the problem, me!

That is not what happened though; Jesus has a plan! His plan is always a whole lot better than we can fathom. Let's back up some though, so you can see how I got to this spot in my life to begin with and how I was given the gift of hope. I'm going to discuss many things including addictions which not only include drug, alcohol, relationships, and entertainment, but also sexual addiction. I will be a little more graphic in this book to bring to light my ways. It's about being transparent. Everyone keeps saying, "There's a time and place and this isn't it." Well, this is the time, and this is the place.

I grew up in Delair, New Jersey. Oh boy! Before I start, I'm going to be as transparent as possible here, so tighten the seatbelts a little bit and show a little grace. I wasn't perfect then and I am not perfect now. I am not the sharpest tool in the shed, but I get by.

I was born in Pennsylvania, on 8th Street in Hunting Park, and our family moved to Delair when I was two years old. I enjoyed where I grew up. I couldn't wait to leave, but I enjoyed it. The seasons there are very noticeable and beautiful when you stop to see and enjoy them, take in the smells and colors of the trees changing, and watch as the different insects come out, like lighting bugs with their glowing bodies. The ground is hard and flat in most areas, but the grass is soft. I now live in Florida, and for some reason the grass here doesn't seem so soft, even on those lawns that are manicured to the nines. I know because I still fall and roll around in the grass from time to time to see if I can feel what I remember from home as a kid. Not that our lawn was perfect. We didn't live like that but a few of our neighbors kept their lawns" tight" and the grass was always soft.

Delair is a small town inside of a township called Pennsauken. Officials there have been trying to remove the name Delair from the map entirely. Hasn't happened yet. It had three areas, one of which had a population that was mostly black, with the other two areas being mostly white. There was also a mix of Asians, Greeks, Indians, Hindis, and Puerto Rican families. At least, that's the way it was when I grew up there. Now it's changed and become more diverse. There was a core group of "Delairians," and our family is part of that group.

Delair had one of the worst reputations, almost as bad as Camden, but it's hard to measure up to the makers of "Hell's Night," as it was called in the newspapers. Whole city blocks were set on fire by the very people who lived there. In Delair, we were proud people, and we were known for being a rough town. You didn't come into Delair and get away with anything. We all knew what was going on around there. Anyone from outside of our town knew we weren't playing. I'll tell you a story that will pretty much sum it up.

I was riding my bike one day and rode like usual across Route 130 from Delair into Pennsauken (even though Delair is in Pennsauken, it was considered different), and I picked a side street that was newly paved to practice my tricks on. I was thirteen at the time. The streets in Delair were rarely repaired or repaved. I had probably been there for thirty minutes or so when a police car came driving up very slowly. I wasn't nervous, frightened, or even suspicious of the cop, but there I was, a white boy in a predominately white neighborhood on a $750.00 Hot Pink GT Pro Freestyle Tour "Team Model" bike. Yeah, that's right, Hot Pink. I was practicing tricks, and the cop stops to ask, "Is that your bike?"

"Yes," I replied, and the officer said, "There's been a report of a stolen bike that matches the description of your bike."

"Really?" I responded (because I can tell you beyond the shadow of a doubt, *no one* had a bike like mine anywhere near Pennsauken).

The officer then asked, "Is your bike registered?"

I said, "Absolutely, I'll flip it over for you to see the numbers!"

As I'm doing that the officer continued, "Do you live around here?"

I said, "Well, actually across the highway in Delair."

The officer replied, "You know nothing good comes from Delair, just drug addicts, thieves, and degenerates! Why don't you go back where you came from, you don't belong around here!"

I'm not joking! Now, looking back, I realize that what was being spoken into my life was horrific. I took it and received it pridefully though, as sick as that might be. I think before that moment I hadn't thought about Delair in that manner, but there it was, that was the way Delair was thought of.

Our house was built on a street that was divided by railroad tracks. I can say I probably "grew up on the wrong side of tracks!" We lived in the house where, when the train went by, the house rumbled a couple times a day and night while sleeping. It's one of those things you just got used to, and most days you didn't even realize it was happening. My friends and I would "hop" trains daily and use the trains to get free rides to different parts of town or even go down into Camden if the Conrail cops didn't catch us. A couple times we even got shot at by shotguns full of rock salt shells. They won't kill you from a distance, but boy does that "sting" stay a while.

One time, I almost had my legs chopped off if not for one of my friends, Bobby, grabbing me and dragging me away from the train as I slipped off the ladder trying to hop a ride. It was a close call, but it didn't slow me down much. We learned how to "run" the cars as well. Many times, the trains would stay stationary for hours at a time for whatever reason, and we would climb the ladders to the tops of the train cars and run along the tops and jump from one car to the next. There were times even when they were moving, we would do this, like in the movies.

There was a wooden train bridge up the street from our house that was used to walk over the train track. We liked to hang out there and get high, drink, climb, make forts, start fires, make out with girlfriends, and whatever. It was one of my favorite places to go and I was devastated when they began to tear it down. The other side of the tracks was considered the river side of the tracks. The Delaware

River comes right past Delair. There are the Walt Whitman, Benjamin Franklin, Betsy Ross, and Tacony/Palmyra bridges, which are the closest to us from what I remember. Since we liked to hang out at the river, we were given the nickname "Delair River Rats." It was a very prestigious and glorious title I might add… *not*!!

The shorelines of the river were nasty, but we swam in the water anyway, digging up treasures like mini cannon balls from the Revolutionary War, old guns, and musket-type rifles. We even found one of those guns in my next-door neighbor's backyard after finding an old water well buried not even three feet in the ground. The well went far down before hitting the water but it's still there today. I gave the gun to my dad, and I think the neighbor's dad wanted it since it was found in his yard, but that didn't happen. After all he was a renter and not the owner.

My elementary school was there, and now it's apartments. My teachers were Mrs. Pennel, Mrs. Ron, Mrs. Fox, Mrs. Kintermils, Mrs. Fantinie, and Mr. Soucup. Oh man, what times we had there! It was a thrill for me to go to school. Learning came easy, and making friends wasn't difficult, but keeping them was a challenge because I had issues. I was a bully in my early years when trying to figure out who I was. I wasn't very good at it either, but I could run my mouth good enough, and I had a very good tough guy persona. It was hard for me at times to back it up because I was truly insecure. I felt inadequate with myself and full of fear, but I was able to mask it.

I was involved in two fights before I was twelve. The first fight was with someone I had been bullying on walks home after school. He came to my brother, Mike, and asked him to get me to fight him. Mike came and got me without telling me it was a fight. He told me we were going to play soccer, and when I finally made it to the park, there was a kid ready to fight me. Well, my true colors were shown that day and all the "sissy boy" came to the surface. I got my butt kicked in front of my friends who I had been manipulating into thinking I was tough. They all saw I wasn't, and it was horrible, humbling, and life changing. That's how it got done though, that's how people found out who you really were in Delair. Put up or shut up. We called it becoming a man. Not true!

The second fight was with a friend in the fifth grade, and we were both almost suspended. It wasn't much of a fight, though. I consider myself the loser because I didn't know how to fight or what to do. Even though I could talk a good game (big mouth), I had none. I even tried karate kicking, which was laughable and considered being a "sissy boy" in those days. I was trying to get a reputation of being a "bad ass" and that was a horrible, horrible way to start. Later, just into my teens, I ran into the first guy again, and I won that time and got to show off to a girl who I always wanted to see me as the "tough guy." That kid and I never talked again.

Delair is close to Cherry Hill, Camden, Cinnaminson, and Palmyra. There was a lot of industry around us. We had chemical plants, a Hess Oil refinery, and warehouses. When I was growing up, there were places to eat, stores to buy groceries, corner candy stores, liquor stores, bars, go-go dancers, and a couple pizza places. At The Pizza Store we would play arcade games like Pacman, Space Invaders, and Ms. Pac-Man. We learned how to break into the machines and give ourselves endless lives, so we didn't have to use quarters. It took a while for the owners to figure it out, but it was fun while it lasted.

Before I became a teen, I was into other things that were much healthier. I got into band and played the trumpet alongside two other male classmates. I was decent, no raw talent, but I could hold my own if there was sheet music around. I played all kinds of sports, mostly football, soccer, and baseball. Football stuck the most, soccer not so much, and baseball I sucked at, more strike outs than hits for sure. I loved the day at the end of the year in elementary school, but I don't remember what it was called. I killed a lot of brain cells over the years. It was always awesome. It was like a "free day" of contests, games, and giveaways. We earned awards, ribbons, played games, won prizes, challenged each other; it was soooo cool. Me and that girl I told you about, the one I always secretly wanted to notice me, were the two fastest people in Delair school at the time. She came close to beating me in relay races, but she was just not quick enough. I think she still thinks she won, but we know the truth!

I don't know exactly how to tell you who I was then, as I changed quite often. The best I can do, I guess, is to describe myself as I remember. I was very skinny, not muscular, and weak compared to my other friends. I always felt inferior, but I could muster up more fake courage than most. I also had "small man" complex. I quickly found out I enjoyed being scared, scared of something physically bad possibly happening to me, but if I had people's attention, I could have died and that would have been fine with me. Dangerous things caught my attention and birthed desire in that area. I wanted to try death-defying-type stuff, and I became an adrenalin junkie very quickly. As a seemingly smaller kid, I wanted to be bigger than life.; bigger than my life, anyway. That was the insecurity and inferiority complex that would kindle the fire for a selfish, self-centered lifestyle, which would eventually fuel my pride and lead me to become the "God of my universe."

The girls had my attention, and I guess I had theirs as well. I asked my preschool teacher out on a date, and it was my first battle with rejection. She was kind and taken back but encouraged me that I was going to have plenty of dates and not to worry about it. I had my first crush in Delair school. My first real kiss wasn't until middle school, although I had a few girlfriends. In elementary school days, they were quick relationships, maybe a couple days or weeks, and sometimes the only relationship was that which we had in school. What I was doing then is considered criminal these days. I was stalking girls, hanging outside their homes for hours waiting for them to come outside, removing girls' skirts right in the middle of class, using obscene gestures throughout school sessions, and touching girls inappropriately without permission. There were games like this that we played constantly. Most of the girls were uncomfortable, I'm sure, but peer pressure was high and before you knew it, everyone who was involved eventually got to be ok with the way things went. Some of the games we played were: 7 Minutes in Heaven, Truth or Dare, and Spin-the-Bottle baby.

I tried to date most of the girls in elementary school, but some I was just friends with. When I got into middle school, I met girls at the Cherry Hill skating rink or Cherry Hill Mall. I didn't like being in a relationship in the beginning, because I saw no need for it. I knew about sex at a young age. I got in trouble in second grade for writing an obscene letter to a new girl in school (turns out she was my best friend's cousin), and her uncle came to the school and threatened me. He got me out of class and held me up by my neck against the lockers. I still pursued her, and that letter was given to my mom by the teacher, who showed it to me and read parts of it to me. Oh, my Lord, it was shameful. I didn't even know what most of it meant. I just repeated what I had heard my older brothers talk about.

When it came to girls and relationships early on, lust was my downfall, but that would change, as all things usually do. I was introduced to pornography through finding a magazine and a deck of cards that had nude women on them in my dad's dresser sock drawer. See, he would put things in there that he took from us kids when we were doing bad stuff with them, like matches or lighters. So, I found these by going through his drawer one day when he was not home. I had never seen anything like that before, and I liked it. A few months later, my dad and I watched a movie, and it showed a woman being raped by a man and there was actual sex happening on the TV. My mom tried to get someone to change it, but my dad said it wouldn't show it again, and it wouldn't get any worse. But the damage was done. I was now seeking out how to see naked women and have sex whenever possible. My fantasies and daydreams were all about women I had seen that day, or I would be at school trying to look up girls' dresses, down their shirts, or even trying to undress them or touch them inappropriately. Today, that's a criminal charge and would be considered sexual harassment.

Without getting into all the details, I have had adult porn in all forms basically at my disposal from magazines, VHS tapes, CDs, and photos. I have been a frequent flyer at strip clubs and gentlemen clubs. I lusted after women whether they or I were in a relationship or not. There are details which I am more "lured" to than others. So lustful perversion goes farther in me than most human beings. I can also lust after cartoon women and can get excited watching them as well. However, whether real or not they have to fit the mold in my mind of what I lust after. That is my "arousal template," which consists of not only size, style, and shape, but also personality, attitude, and ethnicity. I know it's crazy but that's sin, it doesn't make sense, it just is.

> *"Therefore, confess your sins to one another and pray for one another, that you may be healed. The prayer of a righteous person has great power as it is working" (James 5:16 ESV)*

Also, at Delair school, when I was in the second grade, I was strapped to my desk and couldn't leave it. I was only allowed to go to the bathroom. This was a punishment for something I did. I can't even remember what I did now, but I remember I had to kneel and hold books in my hands with my arms spread apart. Things like that are not allowed today. I put dirt in Mr. Soukup's jacket (my fifth-grade teacher) because I got mad at him for benching me during a basketball game. Kickball, parachute, and cart races were the best. Clapping erasers against the outside walls, locking teachers out of the classroom, and playing Pink Floyd's "The Wall" on the record player were priceless school activities. Fun times my friend, fun times.

So basically, my elementary years were exploratory and cool to me. Looking back now I didn't handle myself respectfully towards anyone. I think very differently now. Before getting into middle school, I had made some tight friends and some friendships that would fall to the wayside to make room for new ones. We played outside every day after school, and it was an awesome childhood from my perspective. Coming into my teenage years, I had sexual thoughts about boys as well, but they weren't like the ones I had about girls. Even though I thought one boy was better looking than another, I had no real attraction to them, and I wasn't turned on by them sexually either. I even tried at times to check guys out to see if I could be excited by looking at them, and it just wasn't there. The idea of being homosexual/gay crossed my mind, but there again was one of the many sinful charms the devil would use to try to lure me farther away from God, but that one didn't catch my attention.

Like I said at the beginning, there's a battle going on for our souls, and the devil and God are fighting to win us over. Today, I don't believe it's so much of a battle but more of a strategic course of the *will* of God. After all, He is sovereign and in control of all things, created all things, and works all things out for the good of those who love Him and are called according to His purpose. There is a choice to be made in there somewhere. For those who don't have much of a "church" upbringing, stay with me and maybe you'll get an insight you haven't seen before into the difference between religion and relationship.

I became violently abusive and homophobic toward homosexual boys, and I was attracted to most gay girls. I felt there was more of a lure when I saw two women kissing. Any way of life that was different than the one I was living or was being lived out by my friends was unacceptable to me. Things were very black and white. Believe me, my brothers were not homosexual, and I'm sure my brother, Mike, to this day has no idea I had thoughts about other boys as a kid. I wanted to be like my brothers all the time. I fought inside myself about being racist and prejudiced against other peoples and cultures. I did, however, speak vulgar racist remarks, names, and physically assaulted my share of "different" people. There was a part of me that didn't want to act that way, but I did it to be "part of" something. That was when I made my decision about whether I would be a leader or a follower. It turned out to be a tossup given the circumstances, but I eventually leaned more toward being a leader.

Although my shortcomings showed me all too often how I couldn't possibly be like my brothers, I tried anyway. A scrawny, skinny, cute kid like me, I had been told so often before I was ten how cute I was. I caught on and exploited that quickly to get girls. Being liked by girls really helped me gain popularity. I had "game" in the early years and was not shy at all, but I seemed to get "tight" at all the wrong moments, even before alcohol had any part to play in my life.

Often enough, being the youngest, I missed out on some things when my brothers started driving. My brother Mike is the middle child, I am the youngest, and Chuck is the oldest. I don't know why, or maybe I just like seeing it this way, but Chuck and I had an awesome relationship. We joked a lot together, and he often told me the ways of life as he thought I should know them. He comforted me when I was scared at night, showed me compassion, tried toughening me up when we wrestled, and talked with me. It was a good relationship. I had love for him, looked up to him, and treasured him. Mike and I were ok. We did a lot of the same things, but it was more surface stuff. He was usually showing me up by being cooler than I could ever be and tougher than I could ever be. That's the way I saw it anyway, but we had a pretty good relationship as well. I believe Mike was trying to keep Chuck's attention off me and on him.

We were raised Catholic. Religion is bent more to human behavior as it relates to spiritual beliefs, and I had no religion in me. We were raised in the Catholic faith. Now, what that really means is, we were christened/baptized into the Catholic faith as babies. This is where the sins of Adam and Eve are removed from your life, and you're protected under the faith of your parents until you begin to commit your own sins as you grow then repent for those. We were raised and taught to love and fear God. Jesus was the Son of God (although I didn't get that He was "God"), and he was born from a young virgin girl named Mary, who is known as Mother Mary. Joseph was his father, and he was a carpenter, and we prayed to them and all the saints (Jesus' disciples) during different times in our lives. The devil exists and wants nothing more than to see you perish as quickly as possible or for you to suffer with him in hell for eternity. There's also an upbringing in the church that teaches you about the Bible and all the religious things a Catholic person needs to believe, understand, and learn to do.

We learned those things in something called CCD (Confraternity of Christian Doctrine). The nuns taught us what we needed to learn about the Bible, Jesus, and Catholicism. Now, after you make your First Holy Communion and completed all that learning you were "confirmed," which is the moment you make your own decision to follow Christ. This is equivalent to being "born again," as evangelical Christians call it. I don't know if any

Catholic person when confirmed has any sort of spiritual experience that confirmed for them, they were "saved," but I know of many Christians who have. It seems that in my experience most religious people carry around shame and guilt, as did the Israelites in the Old Testament. Those Christians who have had an experience with Jesus don't seem to carry guilt any longer because He satisfies the once and for all God's debt requirement for their removal. The "born again" believer doesn't do anything to achieve this because he or she understand Jesus did it for them. I believe that's the difference in being born again and just accomplishing religious practices to satisfy a yearning of spirituality of our own doing.

On most Sundays, I was dragged by the ear out the door and told to get in the car for church. I hated it. I didn't pay attention, didn't listen, and didn't want to hear about it. I quickly learned that for most people in our town, going to church was a façade! What a bunch of hypocrites! Maybe some were really trying to do the right thing, I don't really know, and I didn't understand the things they talked about in the church masses. I couldn't make heads or tails out of what they were trying to tell me. I was freaked out by the seemingly haunting organ music. I was more worried about looking cool, being known, and getting noticed by girls. That's what was important to me at the time. In other words, I was already focused on only me!

I didn't even glean any wisdom in the CCD classes I attended for a short period of time before getting kicked out. What got me thrown out of CCD was me giving the nun the finger during one of the classes and telling her off. She escorted me out of the class, and I was told not to return. Now, there's also Saturday confession day. Here's a crazy little idea; I would go into a small dark closet with the priest of the church and speak through this grated window thing. I couldn't see him. He was supposed to be the priest we see every Sunday and I was supposed to tell him all the things I had done wrong or wouldn't tell anyone else and my sins for the week. I knew the Ten Commandments, so I would quickly run through those in my head and be like, "Ok. So, I've stolen candy from the candy store, lied to my parents, I curse, don't pray, and I want this bike that my friend has." The response would be, "Go and say the Act of Contrition ten times, six Hail Mary's, four Our Fathers, and your sins will be forgiven." Then the priest would pray for me through the window, and on my way I would go. That's almost how it would go every time, not that I really remembered my penitence or did them, but you get the drift.

My mom is a die-hard, practicing Catholic, and my dad was Baptist, or Protestant maybe, I don't even know. My dad moved from the church he attended to the Catholic church because my mom wouldn't budge from her religion, and she didn't agree with evangelistic or charismatic views. She thought that most born-again, believing churches, like the one Billy Graham was from, had a "sin and get out of jail free card," so to speak, since Jesus forgave them for their sins once and for all days. She thought this meant they could sin all they wanted, ask for forgiveness, and start all over again. That's the way I think she saw it anyways. So, dad just went along with her because he loved her more. It sort of reminds me of Adam and Eve. I believe Adam showed this sort of disobedience in the Garden of Eden. When Eve ate from the fruit of the tree of good & evil, Adam probably knew it was taking place and didn't stop her but wanted to be with her more than he wanted to be obedient to God. I think it weighed on my dad at times and not only hurt his relationship with us, but with Jesus as well. He didn't share his faith much, and at times he got into arguments with mom about it. Then, they just didn't say much to us.

My dad was the one who prayed at dinner, although my mom sometimes did as well. We didn't pray at every dinner, I don't think so anyways, but at important holiday dinners for sure. Our town had four churches in it. The one we attended was a small, Catholic church downtown called St. Veronica's. I wasn't aware of how different religions could be since I wasn't even interested to begin with. Eventually, I learned that Christians and Catholics considered themselves different, but they believe in the same God, believe that Jesus is God in the flesh, and believe in the Trinity. Where that gets divided is when it comes to salvation, interpretation of doctrine, the books that are included in the Bible, works, and religion.

Although religion and faith weren't important to me, I fought against anyone trying to "preach" or share their faith with me. There was a family in our neighborhood who were born-again Christians. The mother would invite all the kids in Delair to go see Christian movies on the weekends, and she would drive us all in their station wagon across the

Betsy Ross bridge into Philly. I would go occasionally, but not without ulterior motives. Many of my friends and I would sneak out of the movie theater and roam around Philly where the theatre was and get into mischief. We would ring the Liberty Bell by smacking it with pipes or hit it with rocks and then run away. We never stayed to watch the movies, and we eventually got caught and stopped going, but not because we weren't asked to go again. The family members would try to talk to me about Jesus, and I would curse them out. I even tried to hit them or throw stones at them and chase them away. The last thing I wanted to hear about was God. I had such anger toward the idea of God, especially the one of the Bible. Wrapping up religion, I knew there had to be a better way to experience God other than through what I had been taught.

My parents are great parents and people. They sacrificed many things so we could have a great life. None of us are perfect, and they had their faults too, but I'm not pointing them out here. They loved us and did whatever they could do to make sure we were safe, fed, warm, clean, and satisfied. We were raised to be respectful, kind, loving, funny, intelligent, and full of life. What we chose to become is something completely different. I don't blame my parents for anything, although at one time I may have. My behaviors and the choices I made were of my own making and my own doing, or, if you please, my own will. I was not a reflection of my parents. If they could be charged with anything, it would be with being great enablers.

As an Italian woman, my mom didn't like cooking all that much. Go figure! I believed she did for years, and I was into my mom's cooking, and bragged about it behind her back. I don't know why I never told her then, but I have in recent years. She thinks we didn't like her cooking because we were always running out of the house around dinner time. But it wasn't because we didn't want to eat. For me, it was because I was so hyper and intense about going out to play, and as a teen there was too much cocaine in my system, so I couldn't eat. I usually had already made plans to go hang out with friends as soon as my parents were home, but we weren't allowed to go anywhere till after we ate. I learned fast how to sneak food to the dog or hide it in my clothes and get it to the trash can. Sorry mom, I know, I know, what a waste, but we weren't starving and now, knowing what the world outside of Delair was like, we were spoiled. Mom wanted us to sit at the table and talk about our day, to live like a family that cared about what's going on in each other's lives. She was doing what moms should do, uniting her family and helping us know what love looks like.

I would watch movies with my dad like *The Ten Commandments*, *The Robe*, and *The Greatest Story Ever Told*. I liked watching those movies with him because I would see my dad cry at times, and I didn't see him cry that often. I thought to myself, *there is something special about these movies*. I didn't understand what it was, and I was too afraid to ask him about it. My dad wasn't the talking type. Not that I *had* to be afraid, I just didn't know how to talk to him. He was not a violent man and he never hurt us; however, we did receive discipline. We were bent over his knee and spanked or whipped with a belt a few times on our rear end. I was even backhanded one time because I was thought to have cursed while singing a rap song in the car. I don't ever remember being hit out of anger by either of my parents. Not that they didn't get angry; boy let me tell you, mom was known for having a "boomerang shoe." She hit my brother on the back of the head while he was running away from her up the steps. She took her shoe off and threw it at him from the dining room. What a shot that was!

We lived a very average lifestyle. It was not luxurious by any means and maybe some would say we were poor, but it never felt that way to me. My parents were incredible about making our life and our home feel safe and secure, leaving us not wanting for much. They have always been hard-working people, and they instilled that in us boys as well. My mom and I were and are good friends. We spent a lot of time together, especially when we took vacations. Sometimes it would be just my mom and me for a week, maybe two, down to the shore. We would spend all day on the beach. I was a raisin by the time we left, and she still had to drag me off the beach. The waves were so fun, and body surfing was a blast. I even remember my mom getting crushed by a wave as she was yelling at me to get out of the water because I was floating too far downwind from our blanket. While in mid-yell, boom, a white cap taller than her made her disappear, and I watched it come at her. It was *awesome*!

I often helped my mom with cleaning up at home. Sometimes I would even surprise her by dusting, vacuuming, and straightening up before she got home from work. Little did she know it was because I was all jacked up on cocaine. She would read to me at night when I was very little, she took care of me when I was sick, she kissed me daily, and whenever she would tell me, "I love you." The teenage years were much tougher, but it wasn't her fault. I hid myself on the inside, and she lost herself for a while.

One thing about my mom is she never wavered from her faith, her religion, or her family. She relied on hearing from God for direction and strength, and she did what she could to help us see that. She's very proud, humble, direct, and stubborn. It's a very strange mix when it's all coming out at once, but the love she has shown—not only to her family but to her friends and neighbors as well—is noticeable and free. She isn't one to ask for anything in return or hold something over your head. She can speak with a sharp tongue, but I have rarely heard her say a curse word. Mom has always been a picture of God's love, security, comfort, healing, strength, and mercy to me. I love her more than she'll ever experience. I feel the same about my dad. They were great role models and examples of Christ-like love.

I don't want to paint a picture of only the negative aspects of who I was because it wasn't that way, that wouldn't be the truth. I wasn't all bad, and I didn't do all bad things. I made a few good friends growing up and often shared what I had. I had normal fun times like playing board games, going to birthday parties, and bringing gifts that my mom would allow me to pick out at the store. Playing outside with my friends was the best! My favorite activities were climbing trees, playing in the park on the swings and sliding boards, playing basketball and football, and best of all, playing WAR! Man, we took it serious too! We made bunkers, and played in the woods, but sometimes we incorporated the streets. We would get chased away from hiding spots by the neighbors telling us to get out of their yards. Once, we used real BB guns and I got shot in the stomach. It went into my skin and bled. It was awesome!

As teenagers, we played games like "jailbreak," which we took just as seriously as the games we played as little kids. The whole neighborhood was involved and knew when we were playing. Jailbreak was a game that had two teams, cops and prisoners. The cops would seek out and capture the prisoners and bring them to jail where other prisoners, who were still free, could break them out; hence, the name Jailbreak. This could go on for hours, especially when incorporating two or three city blocks to hide in, and most neighbors would allow us to use their properties. We would even hide on roofs and in sheds. We would dress in camo and paint our faces to hide in the woods, it was fun! As everyone got older, the crew got smaller, and we stopped playing. We also stopped teaching the younger ones to play, and it eventually all disappeared.

The town began to change, or maybe I did, and I began to realize I wasn't as dedicated to being a Delairian as I thought I was. Most people don't change their ways, and I was heading down the wrong path seeking out people who were just like I was. But who was I? How was I? Well, I'll tell you. The roots were selfish, insecure, inadequate, prideful (arrogant), shameful, without real remorse, a liar, thief, con-artist, and abusive. On the other side, I was admiring, determined, kind, thoughtful, fun, excitable, daring, foolishly courageous, and enthusiastic. I was a real Dr. Jekyll and Mr. Hyde. When I read that comparison in the book for Alcoholics Anonymous, I almost shut the book to never pick it back up. How did those people know me?

All I have told you so far was to give you background on my life growing up and the family I grew up with.

This next moment, and it was just that, a moment. It changed not only me but my whole family. This is how I recollect the events. It was 1985, so I may not remember all the details clearly.

As I was getting ready to go into middle school in the summer of 1985, our family experienced something that would change our whole family dynamic, my future relationships, and how I thought about the world, God, people, and myself for a very long time. I remember I was sitting playing Atari. My brothers and my grandfather were there, and I heard my brothers talking about going to a lake. I thought I was included but it turned out I wasn't. When they left, I got angry with Chuck because I asked if I could go, and he told me no. Then to avoid me, they snuck out when I was distracted. I got so angry. Later that night, my parents took me and a friend to Cooper River to listen to a string band playing music. We had a place to get out and maybe meet some girls. While we were there, an announcement came over the intercom asking my parents to come to the front area to speak with the police, and that wasn't good. It's never good when you get a call like that at a place like that from the police.

"The police?" my friend asked.

"Yep, that's who wants to talk with my parents," "I think something happened to Chuck!" I continued, not knowing what was about to be revealed. The cop and my dad were standing facing each other as I ran up around the front of the dividing wall from the bleachers. My mother was right next to dad, and I saw dad's knees buckle and his hand stretched out over his face to hide his eyes. My mom got angry and demanded to see Chuck. She was in shock and latched onto my dad as they tried to process what was just announced to them. I ran to them screaming, "What happened? What happened to Chuck?!"

Then my dad cried out, "He drowned!" We grabbed each other, my mom squeezed me so tight, and I lost it. My initial thoughts were *it couldn't be! Not him! Why not Mike?* Yeah, I know, horrible right? Well, I told you I am going to be transparent, and that statement is one I wish I had never thought.

My next thoughts were whispered to me: *God? What God? An invisible tyrant? That is who He must be, not some loving spirit of the universe. If He existed, then that's who he had to be. All the things I hated in myself, I put on God. All of what the priests and nuns said about Him could not be true. It was all a lie! It was false. The Bible must be BS, made up, and make believe. There is no God, there was no flood, I was not created, and He is not watching! If He was, then what the hell was this?!"*

We rushed to the hospital following a police officer. When we got there, we found Mike sitting in a room by himself on a black roll-around chair with no back rest, crying, sobbing like I had never seen before. He grabbed me and hugged me, and we just cried together. He reeked of alcohol! My parents came in demanding to see Chuck. They led us to where his body was laid. There was a cover over him. I don't know who removed the blanket, but there he was. He was blue and stiff to the touch, clammy feeling, but we all touched him, kissed him, hugged him, cried over him, and it was horrible! We just wanted him to get up and breathe, but he didn't. My mom was crying and pleading, "Wake up baby!"

Chuck had drowned and died. They found find him in the water with cattails wrapped around his legs. They pulled him from the water and Mike tried to revive him and so did the medics, but they couldn't. The medics took him to the hospital. We were told they tried to bring him back while in the ambulance as well, but he was DOA(Dead on arrival) at the hospital. The funeral came soon after.

Over 300 people showed up to pay their respects. It was a blur, nonexistent really, and the "after party," or gathering with food, was at the firehall in downtown Delair. I remember walking outside and around the building into the parking lot and screaming into the sky while cursing at God, telling Him, "If You are real, then that means the devil is real, and I will follow him before I'd follow You!" Then I had some other choice words to describe God I'll not repeat here.

Life moved on after Chuck's death. Middle school started, and I was now into bicycle freestyle. Mike joined the Marines and left home, my parents were wrecked, both my brothers were gone, and I felt abandoned and angry. No one was the same after Chuck died. I was only eleven and everyone around me disappeared or checked out. I didn't know what to do, how to cope, or even how to feel. I was often scared of what was going to happen next. Would my parents get divorced? Would they leave me? Would they die? Where would I go? How would I take care of myself? I was lost.

We got a phone call one day that Mike went AWOL and was missing from the military. By that time, more death had come to my family. My godparents, grandparents, and aunt had all died. Mike resurfaced and got booted from the military, then came back home. Death became a normal occurrence, and it wasn't so bad losing someone anymore. I learned how to disconnect from feelings, and with the introduction of alcohol and drugs it became that much easier to just "check out."

At that time, I was into bike freestyle as I have mentioned. I got started because a friend of mine showed me a BMX Plus magazine and said, "You should try doing this stuff." I wasn't very good at riding a bike, but I was daring enough, stupid enough, and crazy enough to try. I liked building things, and just before I turned thirteen, I built my own quarter-pipe ramp in my mother's backyard. I didn't know how to build it, and didn't really have the tools to build it, but I did it anyway. I used hand saws, an electric circular saw, an old hand rotary twist screwdriver, a hammer, nails, and the strength that little old me had. I remember I would get a $10 allowance every week from my parents, and my dad would drive me to the lumber store to get a couple

2 × 4s or 2 × 6s, or maybe a sheet of plywood, so I could put the pieces together as I got them. I found plans on how to build the ramp inside the BMX Plus magazine. I tore the pages out and copied the diagrams, listed instructions, and followed them to the T. Here's the best part: my parents had no idea what they were saying "yes" to when I asked them if I could build the ramp. They weren't expecting a twelve-year-old to build his own ramp, let alone an eight-foot tall, forty-foot-long wooden structure. They thought of a "bike ramp" like you see most kids building from a few pieces of wood and some cinder blocks. When they finally saw what I was doing, my dad said I was going to have to get permission from the county to build something like that. So, we went to the county and he had me show the building department what I wanted to build. They told me I needed to make drawings, a material list, and provide a site drawing of where it was going to be on the property. Then I had to pay some money, and they would decide if I could do it. They finally decided to approve it, and I got to build my ramp.

People, Places & Things

People, Places & Things

At that time, my mother's dad lived with us. My grandfather drank alcohol daily until he died in his nineties. He was such a riot at times, and we had fun messing with him. For example, in the middle of the day, he liked to go outside and pick through mom's garden to find rotten tomatoes and throw them into the woods. So, if we happened to be playing in that area when he did, we would find them and throw them back up at him out of the woods. We would be quiet as he yelled and tried to find out who was throwing them back at him. One day, he sat down on the steps with me in front of the house and made a deal with me. He said that before he died, he would help me buy my Pink GT, the one I told you about earlier. I would have to get half the money and then he would provide the other half.

Two years later, it was my first day of ninth grade, and I had a road rash on my face from falling on the quarter pipe in my back yard. That was a "tough guy" moment for me. I had just gotten sponsored by Peregrine Bikes and was trying a "No Footed Air," about six feet out (nothing big), on a bike I hadn't ridden before. I had just put it together right from the box, and something went wrong. I slammed down and was knocked out cold on the flats. My neighbor found me and woke me up. My mom had just pulled up to the house as I went running into the bathroom with a bloody face. She helped clean me up, and the thought came to me, *I'll stop riding if I don't go back out there now and ride that ramp while I'm still hurting.* So, that's what I did. I went back outside, jumped on my bike, and took one charge at the pipe, shaking scared, still bloody and bleeding, high enough to feel the adrenaline. When done, I ran back inside to finish having the cuts cleaned up and bandages put on.

That was my first lesson on facing my fears for real. That moment showed me I had no fear. There wasn't anything I wouldn't try at first. I would do whatever, whenever, and I rode that wave for a long time. I got my street creds, and they called me "Little Crazy Seabolt" for the longest time. The biking thing got me notoriety around the township. I won some contests and was named in a magazine but with no photos, because it was my worst performance ever. I was beaten out by a young Dave Mira, later X-Games Champion, who became a legend.

People, Places & Things

My arrogance level at that time was off the charts, but it was all false pride. I often flaunted my talents in front of those less talented. I loved riding though; riding on my own without anyone around was the best. Learning and trying new tricks to show others later was what I liked so much. I really enjoyed performing, but I was anxious most of the time. My arrogance often got the best of me and that was frustrating. Thinking about the competition I lost at the Masters (Bike Freestyle Competition) was devasting to me. I was not a good loser. It showed me once again that I had no raw talent; just like the trumpet, I just learned stuff. My insecurities were showing themselves, and drugs were now glaringly more alluring and became excessive quick. I began using drugs frequently right away. It didn't take weeks or months to have a desire to use drugs, it was instantaneous. This sinful charm the devil lured me in with stuck!

Not long after Chuck died, I smoked my first joint with a kid who was a little older than I. It was just after getting into the bike thing. We were in the woods near the "Rocks" before there were homes built there. The Rocks was the place to hang out and while there, I would often try to climb up them from street level. They were the remnants of an old train walkover that once went through our town in that same location. Once I conquered the Rocks, I felt accomplished. Later, while watching Alex climb, I remembered those moments and related to him.

After we smoked the joint, I remember going to my friend's house, knocking on the door, seeing him sitting in the living room, and yelling, "Yo, I just smoked my first joint!" as I began to laugh. My friend said, "Shut up, stupid, my mom is in the kitchen!" That was the start of my partying.

I had already drunk alcohol at a New Year's Eve party before Chuck died, so I knew the effects, but this was different. I really liked pot. Many more of those times would come, and many more drugs would come. Cocaine, acid, and mushrooms were the things I preferred most. Eventually, crack cocaine would consume me more than I could consume it! Those were the drugs of choice for me. Let me tell you, they were not in short supply. I also took pills, and snorted heroin. No matter what drugs were around I was good with. I wouldn't use needles. No shooting galleries for me. On occasions I've had enough drugs in me at one time to kill a few people and I didn't overdose. Most would have lost their minds or died because of the number of drugs and amounts I was consuming.

My introduction to alcohol was through my grandfather and a couple of parties my parents threw. I was named after my grandfather, and he drank a lot. He would walk around the house sometimes making 7 and 7s and wouldn't know if he spilled it or drank it, so he would just go make another one. He didn't know that sometimes I got to it first. No one ever found out I was tasting them. Curiosity is what had me pick up that first drink. It was innocent enough, and there was no damage done. The first time I got drunk was with my best friend and blood brother Johnny. We had a bottle of Jack Daniels and walked down the tracks to Bums Cave. Bums Cave was a dug-out hole in the ground that went underneath the railroad tracks where bums would live. At that time no one was there, and we drank a bottle of Jack Daniels. I never threw my guts up so much before. It was the worst feeling I had ever experienced, dry heaves, spinning, and falling, oh man! When it was all said and done, I thought I wouldn't ever do it again. Until I drank something different and didn't get sick, now I can drink *and* hold my liquor. Black Sambuca and Southern Comfort were my favorites, besides rum.

Once, when I was at a concert, I was given a 16-ounce glass full of Jack Daniels and no ice. It was warm to say the least, but since I was halfcocked already, I downed it. I passed out right at the beginning of the concert and regained consciousness right at the end. Dang, I hated it when that happened. Why did I ever pick up alcohol again? Change. I wanted to be, feel, think, act, sound, and look different. In my head, alcohol was going to do it for me. It was my solution to the problem. Most times when I drank, I thought it had done its job and really worked. I started to have a new confidence. When I looked in the mirror, I saw someone different. I began to think differently, and I was becoming who I wanted to be. Who was that? Not me, just different. I was changing, or so I thought.

Once I smoked that first joint though, it was different, I really liked it. I was in middle school and getting ready for high school. I was popular, getting girls, and having fun without a care in the world. I was going to school and buying drugs there. I was getting good grades because I cheated well, going to freestyle bike contests, putting on bike shows, doing State Fairs, putting on shows at dance clubs, having tons of people over to ride my ramp daily, and I even had a friend take a small video to send out to bike companies. As you already know, I got sponsored, but not only by a bike company, by Oakley glasses as well! I was "living large."

The parties were happening all the time it seemed. Every weekend someone threw a party somewhere. I was a head-banger metal head with long hair in those days. In Delair, if not at someone's house, parties were one of four places: Dago's Point, The Pit, The Trestle, or The Corner. One way in and one way out. My brother, Mike, and I once had to carry a keg from The Trestle back to The Corner, which was not even two houses from home. At The Corner we had fights, lit cars on fire, and consumed massive amounts of drugs and alcohol. You see, during that time in that town there was a mutual respect of sorts between us and the cops. At times, if they had a problem with you, they would take their badge and gun off and fist fight, right there in the street. Things got settled that way, not always, but at certain times with certain people. With a cop, it was always one on one till someone gave up or it was obvious who won, and it just stopped. No one got shot, no cops got killed, and neither did any of us.

The fires down at The Pit were something to remember. There were so many good times. "Stand back Dego, I'm goanna give you a crew cut," a friend said as he leaned in to light a pile of loose gun powder he had just poured out on the ground. Can you say, "YAHOO SERIOUS"? The guy's face and hair went up faster than "D" (my best friend's older brother) could say "Nooo Bill, don't do it!" RIP Bill! He didn't die that night. My friends threw a jacket over his face and patted him out. He recovered and didn't change a bit afterward; he was still just as crazy as ever.

A few years later, I was at a State Fair with a friend and watched as he threw an empty whiskey bottle into a full crowd of people hoping to start a fight while we were waiting to hear a concert, and it hit somebody. Six cops later, he was in Cherry Hill Police Department locked up for drunk and disorderly. He played cards with them while he waited to get bailed out by his mom. I am not kidding. You think that doesn't sound like a good time? Well, it was for me.

During my middle school years, I was taken advantage of by an older woman who was probably in her twenties and lived with a friend of mine. I was drunk at a sleep over at his house. I was dancing to music by myself, and she began to dance with me. Before I knew it, we were having sex standing up. Now, I've only slept with four girls in my life, if that tells you anything. Not that I didn't try to sleep with more (remember I wasn't a Christian at that time), but the effort was not good. My game sucked and just having sex wasn't all that important to me. I truly enjoyed the hunt, the playfulness, the relationship more than the actual sex part. Listen, when a girl says, "That's it?" when sex is over, believe me it's not good. Things got better in that area, not much better, but it's progress not perfection. I didn't know it then, but I was trying to fill the loss of the relationship with my brother with women. I eventually became a woman's worst nightmare... *needy*!

I noticed one girl in the seventh grade, whom I would later meet in the summer between middle and high school. She would become my first "real" relationship. I was "in love" with her, no doubt, to the extent of knowing what love was or felt like at that point. It turned out to be more of an obsession though. My brother says she's the reason I stopped biking, but that is a half-truth. I was more in love with drugs and drinking than I was with her. She wasn't the first girl I slept with, but she was the first one that meant something.

God made a way past all that happened with that relationship, and I'm going to be obedient to His lead here. When we met, I was fourteen years old, my biking had started to take off, and things were looking bright. But with all the drugs and drinking, it wasn't going to last. I remember in high school that a man named Toma came to our school to talk about drug addiction, recovery, and the like. At that time, I had some issues come up through my behavior while intoxicated that were not good. I was becoming violent when drunk; acid use was off the charts, and bad trips were happening quite frequently. I choked my girlfriend once, not to death of course, but I choked her. When I drank, I got angry and violent. There was lots of pushing and rough grabbing. When I found out my girlfriend was pregnant, I told her I would like to have a child, and that we would make great parents. I thought maybe it was just what I needed to get me on the right track. I also told her I would be ok with whatever decision she made. When she decided to have an abortion, I was nothing but cruel to her, even though I said I would support whatever decision she made.

I remember a time when I was on LSD and I almost lost it completely, mentally. I heard stories of people never coming back from an LSD trip and being locked up in insane asylums. That's what some of my friends thought was going to happen to me one night while tripping. The hits we all took were the size of postage stamps and were very strong. I wound up taking two of them and once it kicked in, I knew I was in trouble. Even though I had tripped in the past, that was the first time I dropped acid while having anxiety already in place. I had been fighting with my girlfriend, and I was hiding out from her to be with my friends. Before I knew it, I was tripping so hard that the earth seemed to be bending and shifting in ways I had never experienced before, not to mention how colorful everything got and how real the hallucinations seemed. I only remember bits and pieces, but from what was told to me by some friends, it was horrible to think I wasn't coming out of it. At one point, I thought I saw my girlfriend walking down through one of the trails back at the river, but it wasn't her at all it was my best friend. I hugged and tried to kiss her, which was him, and still can't live that one down to this very day. I couldn't seem to form an intelligent sentence or speak clearly. I think it could be interpreted as "speaking in tongues," but others say it was just gibberish.

Remember when I said earlier there was a "battle for our soul"? I remember that I saw God as this huge bright light that covered the entire sky from horizon to horizon, and I had to turn my head away. I remember hearing a voice come from above (God) and one from underneath me (the devil), and they were discussing me as I laid on the earth, which at that point opened underneath me and became a grill grate (like in a BBQ grill). Fire shot up through the grate past me. It felt like I was being burned like a hamburger, but it was all a hallucination… or was it? In that conversation between God and the devil, I only remember God saying, "He isn't yours, he's mine." This became very important later.

Maybe it wasn't just a hallucination after all. My friends had to take care of me that entire night while they were on LSD also. They took turns watching me and staying with me so that I didn't hurt myself, or anyone else for that matter. I had already punched a Puerto Rican guy, who was a drug dealer, in the face, and he almost wound up shooting me. I don't know if they had to take me home, but I woke up under a bed in my friend's house and had no recollection of the night before. They were just happy to see I was alive, coherent, and speaking normally.

My personality was never the same after that night and none of my relationships were either. People didn't look at me the same after that or treat me the same. It was devastating. It didn't stop me from using drugs though. I would later drop over twelve hits of acid at one time with another best friend of mine, while I was high on crack. His steps became escalators, and the floors became like water. Once I was dropped off at school in the eleventh grade, in time for homeroom, by a couple of much older friends after being out all-night doing cocaine. I had cocaine in my pocket, and they thought it was the funniest thing they had done in a while. Another time, I bought crack cocaine while on PCP in Camden without realizing I did it. I was nearly shot twice in Camden while buying crack. Once I was robbed at gun point with the gun to my temple and the guy said, "I should blow your head off white boy." Little did he know I was thinking, *get it done, bro. You'd be doing me a favor.* That was when drug use really started to overshadow drinking. Let me back up again though.

When Toma came (the drug and alcohol speaker back in Pennsauken High School), I got involved with our school addictions counselor, who would allow us to smoke cigarettes in her office. We would be able to get out of eighth-period class once a month to go to an AA meeting at a hospital. I was introduced to the Twelve Steps and recovery at that time. If we volunteered, we could go speak to an elementary school class about staying away from drugs and alcohol. Yeah, I tried it. I lied to those kids when they asked me if I had tried the stuff. I never went back to that counseling class. I fled the scene because I was going to be found out and confronted about being a fraud and a liar. I didn't want to lie to the kids. What they thought about me mattered at that time and I didn't want them to see me as I saw myself—a loser! Besides, I wasn't trying to stay sober, and I can't give away what I don't have.

The inner turmoil, even at fourteen, was horrible—constant mental battles over being worthy to be liked, loved, and accepted. Religion didn't help. According to religion, God couldn't or wouldn't like, love, or accept me the way I was. I had to clean up and straighten up, and I couldn't do that. I couldn't stop thinking so lustfully, and my violence toward others was glaring. How could anyone else accept me if God wouldn't? I didn't like me, I didn't love me, and I didn't accept me either. Even then I couldn't measure up to my own standards much less someone else's standards, so how could I measure up to God's standards? After all, I was thinking I was God, so there wasn't anything to do about it anyway.

A newspaper article was written about me and my girlfriend and our drug use as teens after an interview with a news reporter at the school. We told her some things that made her scratch her head, that's for sure. Who wouldn't be confused after listening to a fourteen-year-old telling all these types of stories? I left the biking scene because of a bruised ego, hoping to start a new life with my girlfriend, and I didn't really look back. It wasn't going to work anyway because I was missing that raw talent like I mentioned before. I stopped playing sports in high school, and I just became a party guy. I was told I would have to cut my hair if I was going to play football and that wasn't going to happen. After all, girls loved my hair. A coach approached me and asked me to be on the running team too. There was no way I would have been thought of as a chump by my friends. That was another moment I should have taken advantage of, but my reputation was more important.

Drivers Ed class? Yep, we had it. I took it and passed it. How might you ask? Well, during one of our days out to test drive, our instructor, who just so happened to be the school football coach, decided to have us drive him to the liquor store during the class. Yep, so don't you know who just so happened to be in the car at the time? One of the football players (whose name will remain secret) got into the driver's seat. Once the coach was in the store, we took off in the Drivers Ed car. Talk about one of the funniest and scariest joy rides, as we weren't sure how the coach was going to react. But what could he say, we had him dead to rights, and he was our pass for the class to go get our licenses. I was so reckless at that time. Once, while waiting for the teacher to arrive one day before we went driving, I had a schoolmate watch out for me while I chopped out a line of coke right there in the coach's office. I just didn't care!

There were a few more fights I would get into. We Delairians, who were tight, had a rumble one time where we loaded up a couple cars full of people and drove out to back up one of our friends who was going to fight another guy from Pennsauken. They must have known about it because twenty guys came pouring out of the house. None of us expected it, and we all turned and started to run the other way. One of my friends then stopped, tore off a fence picket, and headed back toward the mob. We all turned and started running back toward the mob, and it was on! Everyone was swinging, getting kicked, hit with pipes, bats, and brass knuckles. It was a true rumble. I remember getting away from one fight only to get into another one, and when I turned, I only saw a bat swinging for my head and then an arm came into view. My brother, Mike, moved in between me and the bat and took the strike. He kicked the dude's butt right there in front of me. It was awesome!

Another time, friends from Pennsauken came to Mr. Hendricks' house for a party, and we all wound up fighting because of a beer run mix-up. We had all chipped in money for alcohol, and when the delivery came back, there was only one case that someone was hogging. Well, I went over and removed two six packs of bottles from the case and started to run away, and the guy, whoever he was, started chasing me. My best friend stood in the way and there it was. Immediately, the whole party began to fight each other. We were so closely piled on top of one another that we took down the chain link fence separating the yards. I remember a friend of mine showing me his eye, and he said that I hit him. I didn't even know it was him. Everyone eventually got tired enough and the cops were on their way, so everyone split. After that night, I learned to choose my battles, pick my fights wisely, and know when not to engage. That is, unless I had too much alcohol; then there was no fear and no anxiety. Alcohol made me feel ten feet tall and bulletproof.

Chapter 2
Experience

"For because he himself has suffered when tempted, he is able to help those who are being tempted." (Hebrews 2:18 ESV)

Crack was the epidemic of the 1980s. People were getting hooked on "Ice" and losing their minds. I was not far behind. Before I turned twenty-one, I was a full-blown crackhead. Nothing else mattered. The only thing on my mind that was important was how to get more money for more crack. That's it. I would steal from my parents, my brother, my employers, and my friends. It didn't matter if I could get away with it or not. I'd even play it off and help people look for the very things I stole. It's hard for me to remember some moments, and the loss still hurts inside. Drugs have blotted out memories of my brother Chuck, my mom, and other family members. I have some memories of Mike. I wanted to be closer to him. He and I were not so close, and

I told myself getting closer to him wouldn't matter because if he were to die, it wouldn't hurt as bad. That's not true though, I loved him just as much as I loved Chuck, but that was how I thought I needed to guard myself. I tried to put distance between myself and things I was passionate about. I didn't want to feel love, but that love was the very reason I should have been involved with them. Giving of myself is what love looks like, and I didn't do that when I should have, because to love was to lose what I loved… myself! It is still a battle inside me to this day. Christians call it, "dying to self" daily.

Working came easily for me. I was dependable, self-motivated, and ambitious in the beginning. But eventually, drinking and drugging would interfere with every job I acquired. I became known as "No Show Joe." I even had a boss who would cover my tracks sometimes because I was at least good at my job. I have done a lot of different jobs, mostly construction: electrical, framing, remodeling, painting, tiles, flooring, block, stucco, roofing, trim work, you name it. I was a sponge too, and always seemed to get the bosses who said they could see themselves in me for some reason (this is God). Because of this, they would begin to really teach me their trades.

This would become very useful later, as would all my job skills.

Warehousing was something I thrived in as well. I even worked for a place while in co-op class in high school. The company would eventually fire all my other coworkers but me. Then, after I quit that job to move on, my mom was able to use me as a reference to get hired there and became very well liked and honored. She worked there until her retirement.

I used cocaine frequently while in high school and on the job. I remember one specific day very well. It was 1993. Mike and I were sniffing lines down in the basement, and I was getting ready to make another run to get more. The only thing available was crack, so I bought it and brought it back. We together learned how to smoke crack. I couldn't stop, and I couldn't stop drinking either. I tried all the usual tricks to decrease my drinking: no weekday drinking, no weekend drinking, only drinking beer, just drinking shots, never in the morning, never after 11 p.m., only wine, not mixing beer and whiskey, only smoking crack and not drinking, the list went on and on. Nothing ever worked the way I expected, and nothing ever changed the way I felt about myself on the inside or helped with the guilt of what I was doing to others and myself. The guilt and shame I had were heavy. I was ashamed of who I was and what I was. I didn't have any delusions of being a good person. I wasn't. I was a bad person.

I quit drinking and drugging many times over the years, but it never lasted more than two weeks, if that. Sometimes it would only last one day. I swore it off and made promises to myself and others. I would scream at the sky and to God, "You made me this way so change me!" I even prayed it away at times, but nothing ever changed, most importantly, because *I* never changed. The desire to feel different or be different was always looming over me. These are some thoughts that constantly ran through my head.

You'll never be good enough.
You can't quit.
You'll always be a piece of #%&*.
No one really loves you anyway.
You can't measure up
You're a waste of time.
Trying never helped anyone.
You're worthless and useless.
God doesn't even know you exist.
God could never love you.

Just slit your throat and get it over with.
You can't change, it's impossible.
You'll always be a loser.
Things will never be ok.
You're better off without anyone.
You'll never fit in
You are not normal.
You're a horrible person

On January 2, 1996, I turned myself into rehab for drug and alcohol treatment. Well, God showed me to the door, but I didn't see it that way. I was not accepted for in-patient because I wasn't what was considered "dependent" to alcohol or in need of detox from heroin. I was just a cocaine/crackhead junkie, so instead I got "out-patient" therapy four days a week, or something like that. That day was the greatest day of my life besides becoming a dad, and getting saved, but I didn't know it at the time. I met the love of my life that day as well. It was real love as I didn't know what love is. Jesus brought us together at this moment against all worldly recommendations.

There was a girl named Stacey and one day she asked me to come over to her house, and I accepted the invitation. Yep, that's right, rehab love. It was incredible, crazy, sinful, lustful, exciting, wrong, unhealthy, dangerous, fun, amazing, scary, debilitating, scornful, full of drama and strife, and just what I needed! There were memorable days, nights, and events. Rehab was forgetful but being back in those rooms at AA meetings was different that time. I could often relate to what people were sharing in those meetings, and things started to stick with me. I would think about the sayings I heard like, "First Things First"; "One meeting a week, makes One WEAK"; and "Keep coming back until the miracle happens." I would ponder them, really think about them, then drink or use. When I would go back, they would welcome me and say, "Keep coming back," I wanted to punch one of them and tell them to just shut up! Lord knows, I hated hearing it every time.

My habits didn't change, my thinking didn't change, my behaviors didn't change, and my heart didn't change. Nothing on the outside was really changing except I was getting older. That is not to say I did everything I was supposed to, such as don't get into a relationship within the first year, don't use, don't drink, call people in recovery before you pick up, and go to a meeting every day. I didn't listen. I was still trying to figure it out. I had to find the answer to why I kept using and drinking dangerously. I was sure I was the "exception" to the rule. I was sure that one day I would be able to drink like a normal person. "Once an alcoholic always an alcoholic" didn't apply to me. That's where the problem was. Why couldn't I drink or use it safely? Anger or rage was starting to be the only emotion I could understand—it would come out instead of hurt or sadness—which only produced more pain because of the repercussions of my behavior toward others.

Stacey and I went back and forth a little during that time. I was convinced to try to do what was being asked of me and call off the relationship. She would get involved with a couple of different guys, but nothing really came of any of it. Then we would get back together, or one of us would use and the other would follow suit, and neither one of us would stay sober. Just like the counselors and people in AA said would happen, "Two sickies don't make a wellie." That's what they said in the rooms. They said we wouldn't focus on ourselves like we should. We would be more focused on the relationship and our own selfish desires, and we were. To be perfectly honest, we had some awesome times though. We had moments when all the hair on my body stood straight up. These were good moments just being together while not intoxicated. The intoxicated times, or the times when we were using, were the rough and not so fun times.

We were doing our best to stay sober while driving in her Mustang one night. I didn't own a car at the time. We were driving wherever, and we just drove and talked and got lost. We wound up running into a dead end at the shore. We got out of the car and walked over a wooden walkway and there was the ocean. It was beautiful and we were in awe of it! It was a magical moment. I picked up a tennis ball that was lying in the sand and wrote "Beach Night 1996" on it for a keepsake. I believe the tennis ball is still in our home to this day somewhere. During one of the times, we separated, and she came to my house in Delair to meet up with me before taking off again somewhere. She had told me she was going to be leaving and wasn't sure when we might see each other again. I got this overwhelming feeling that if I didn't convince her to stay with me that day, we might not ever see each other again. "I don't completely understand why, but if you leave, I feel we are never going to see each other again and that just can't happen. So please, whatever you do today, just don't to why I kept using and drinking dangerously. I was sure I was the "exception" to the rule. I was sure that one day I would be able to drink like a normal person. "Once an alcoholic always an alcoholic" didn't apply to me. That's where the problem was. Why couldn't I drink or use it safely? Anger or rage was starting to be the only emotion I could understand—it would come out instead of hurt or sadness—which only produced more pain because of the repercussions of my behavior toward others.

Stacey and I went back and forth a little during that time. I was convinced to try to do what was being asked of me and call off the relationship. She would get involved with a couple of different guys, but nothing really came of any of it. Then we would get back together, or one of us would use and the other would follow suit, and neither one of us would stay sober. Just like the counselors and people in AA said would happen, "Two sickies don't make a wellie." That's what they said in the rooms. They said we wouldn't focus on ourselves like we should. We would be more focused on the relationship and our own selfish desires, and we were. To be perfectly honest, we had some awesome times though. We had moments when all the hair on my body stood straight up. These were good moments just being together while not intoxicated. The intoxicated times, or the times when we were using, were the rough and not so fun times.

We were doing our best to stay sober while driving in her Mustang one night. I didn't own a car at the time. We were driving wherever, and we just drove and talked and got lost. We wound up running into a dead end at the shore. We got out of the car and walked over a wooden walkway and there was the ocean. It was beautiful and we were in awe of it! It was a magical moment. I picked up a tennis ball that was lying in the sand and wrote "Beach Night 1996" on it for a keepsake. I believe the tennis ball is still in our home to this day somewhere. During one of the times, we separated, and she came to my house in Delair to meet up with me before taking off again somewhere. She had told me she was going to be leaving and wasn't sure when we might see each other again. I got this overwhelming feeling that if I didn't convince her to stay with me that day, we might not ever see each other again. "I don't completely understand why, but if you leave, I feel we are never going to see each other again and that just can't happen. So please, whatever you do today, just don't leave and stay with me," I told her. Reluctantly, she stayed, and we continued our relationship.

One day after relapsing once again. I drove in Stacey's car out to South Street, PA. I knew of a shop there where I could buy Nitrous oxide canisters to use as "Whip Its". This is where you put these small canisters into what's called a "cracker" to puncture the whip it, which will then fill up a ballon with the gas. You then inhale the gas out of the ballon and get high off the gas. Which sometimes can cause you to pass out. This is the same stuff they give you at the dentist to be sedated during your visit if requested.

I am driving back to Berlin, NJ in Stacey's red mustang and I have decided I'm going to get high while driving using the whip its. I get one set up and the balloon is full, as I begin to inhale the ballon and feel euphoria, I remember slowing down for a red light and then waking up with a house attached to the front of the mustang. I began to immediately try to put the car in reverse to move it away from the house, but it wasn't going anywhere. I then hear a knock on the window and this woman yelling at me to turn the car off and asking if I'm ok? I rolled the window down, shut off the car and started to understand what had happened. This woman says,

"The police are on their way" and then tells me I crashed into her daughter's room, but no one is hurt. I asked if I could use the phone to call my girlfriend and let her know what was happening and she agreed. I called Stacey and tell her she'll need to come get me and where I was. Within minutes of that call, an officer shows up and I go to meet him at his patrol car. He does his job and finds out what's going on. Takes my license and runs it, it's clean and then he looks at me with a smile on his face, hands me a trash bag and says, "I having the car removed and towed. If there's anything in that vehicle that shouldn't be there or you want to take with you, I suggest you go it now before I search it!" Unbelievable right? Yep, this is how things happened in my life which only told me and allowed me to continue to do things that should be done. My mind told me all I had to do was own up to my mistakes and they would work themselves out. Stacey and her mom showed up to the scene, spoke with the deputy and we left the scene with a ticket for running a red light.

Just before the cop showed up, I was able to speak with this old guy who was sitting out on his front porch enjoying his coffee before the accident. He witnessed what happened and told me that I stopped at the red light and then blew through the red light coming straight at him and his house when the car hit a curb and spun around in the other direction. Accelerated, hit another curb, went airborne through some bushes and then landed in the yard of the house the car eventually ran into and stopped. I had blacked out behind the wheel after ingesting the whip it. I lost consciousness and never knew a thing until I woke up. Another moment where God has his hand not only on my life but the life of an infant baby girl who was sleeping in the room where Stacey's car came to rest at that day.

In 1997, we moved to Florida for a geographical change and to help move Stacey's mother there. We both thought that maybe things would be different, but that is not the case when you bring or take "yourself" with you. At least, that was my experience anyway. I sought out all the same things, people, and places. Crack was an easy access item where we lived, and I found it fast. I began to get into trouble with law enforcement quickly, as the police weren't the "hometown" cops I was used to, and they dealt with me differently.

Within two months of moving to Florida, I had been arrested for two counts of aggravated battery, assault with a deadly weapon with severe harm and disfigurement to a human, and DUI. I wound up getting into a fight at a Christmas party we were invited to by someone Stacey knew. I'll leave all the details out, but I used a beer bottle as a weapon and cut a man's face pretty good. I was out of control and my pride was leading me. A month or two after that, I followed a girl home from a dance club in Port Richey and got pulled over for tailgating and arrested for DUI. I was cheating on Stacey that night.

At the end of 1998, Stacey was pregnant, and I got arrested for violating my community control probation with new cocaine and paraphernalia possession charges. While in county jail, my daughter, Danielle, was born without her father there to welcome her into this world. Stacey's mother and my mother were with her, but there was no man by her side. That divide carried through in both my relationships with Stacey and my daughter for years to come. They brought Danielle to see me while I was in the county jail. You know that classic movie shot of people putting their hands up on opposite sides of glass in the same spot to touch each other as a sign of love for one another? Well, that's how I got to see my daughter for the first time. I couldn't even process it. She looked like a doll. My dad also saw me through that glass and got up out of his seat and walked away. That moment stuck with me, but at the time I couldn't show any emotion about it at all for it would have shown weakness. So, I did what I did best and buried it immediately. I knew he loved me, but inside, I believed he saw me as I was: a thief, a drug addict, a liar, a selfish person who only ever thought about himself, rather than as a loving person, a loving son, or even a decent person for that matter. Maybe he was even thinking about how he may have been a failure as a father? I don't know. It tore me up inside and he was a great father.

My disconnect with my family and my daughter was very noticeable, but becoming a father didn't derail any of my addictive behaviors, thoughts, or actions. Some men have said that when they had a child everything changed. Not for me. I seemed to welcome parenting as just another responsibility that prevented me from partying. I had no sense of guidance toward my daughter, and I had no empathy or compassion toward my girlfriend as a new mother. I just saw it as an inconvenience to my drinking and enjoying my life. Once again, I didn't know how to love anyone. Doesn't seem the learning to love is happening right?

I pled with the court system to allow me to go to treatment for alcohol and drug abuse. There was a process to go through to get accepted into the treatment center. They didn't take just anyone at Daytop and the court didn't try to send you there unless your attorney asked for it. There was a gentleman who came to visit with me while in the Pasco County jail, which is behind the courthouse in New Port Richey, Florida. He asked me a few questions, then he asked me to tell him a little about myself and why I was looking for treatment. I don't remember what I said but it was a bunch of fluff. He saw right through it and told me, "You ain't ready" and began to walk away. I panicked and said, "Wait, what do I have to do? What do you want me to do?" He stopped, turned around, and asked, "What are you willing to do?" At that point I was willing to do anything, he asked if it meant staying away from prison. He looked at me with a smile on his face and said, "Stand on your head." So, I did. Then I stood back up and he walked closer to me and shook my hand and said, "You got your recommendation."

I went to sentencing and was awarded treatment, but my original sentence was still in force. Four months later, I took a van ride to a treatment center in Ocala, known then as Daytop. Today it's known as Phoenix House. When I was there it was a twenty-four-month program. It was designed as a therapeutic community that had staff and volunteers, but the residents were the ones who took care of the facility operations. There were job functions that consisted of things like housekeeping, kitchen, phones, security (although there was another name for it to not use lingo like police or security, but that is what it was), and education. Also, residents had to attend groups, counseling classes, and one-on-one sessions. We were able to leave the facility for things like AA meetings, education-related training, and medical reasons. No visits were allowed until you were there at least six months with no incidents.

Residents there had charges like murder, theft, drug- and alcohol-related manslaughters, and rape (both child and adult). Most everyone was facing a good amount of prison time, and this was the last stop, the last chance to learn to be different. I got a lot from that place; it broke through my pride and helped me to be more humble and less aggressive. I reacted a lot. I wanted to use my hands in confrontation and scold people with my words. They helped break me off from those things for the most part. I knew all of that would go out the window if I were to drink or use it again. While there, I had to wear a sign that said "Confront Me" on my chest. I couldn't talk back to whoever came up and confronted me. I had to just stand there and listen to them. It was difficult to say the least. It brought me to tears at times because I couldn't do anything, and eventually it helped me to see I didn't have to retaliate. I recognized that words hurt, and I had the power to choose how to respond to them. One morning, I forgot to make up my bunk and had a consequence of bringing my wooden bunk from my dorm and putting it up on stage for morning meeting to show and explain to everyone how to make up a bunk. I did this in front of 150 residents. Embarrassing? Yes! Humbling? Of course! There were also residents who were there as "Private Pay." Those were usually young people over eighteen whose parents were paying to have them there to get help. Sometimes there was a person who could afford to do it on their own who checked themselves in to get help.

I was a dead-beat dad, horrible boyfriend, and a poor image of a father for any child. I blamed God. After all, supposedly He made me, so He must have made me this way, and He wouldn't change me! Obviously, He must not see me or the things I was doing because He would have stopped me, right? Prod me into submission maybe. Strike me down before I killed someone who cared for me or who I cared about, since I was unable to care for anyone anyway. Love is not a feeling, it's an action. You know someone loves you not because of what they say or by how many times they say it, but because of what they do, how they treat you, and what they are willing to sacrifice for you.

My brother Mike came to live with us in Florida for a while, and there are three incidents that stick out to me during that time. The first one is when I took Mike out to have a good time and wanted him to see the causeways and how awesome they looked at night. Well, Mike's brain told him something different and he started to yell at me for bringing him to the water! We were drunk and he was using morphine at the time, which I didn't know. He suddenly ran from the beach into the water and started to swim out. He probably got about twenty yards out, then I saw him stand up. It's very shallow water along the causeways, except for a few spots. Within a few minutes he was out of sight, and we couldn't find him. Stacey and I drove up and down the causeway for at least an hour and he didn't turn up. Did something happen to him? Did he drown himself in the Gulf? I didn't know, so we went home. We didn't call the police because we thought maybe he'd turn up later or the next day. Inside I felt like it didn't really matter. I didn't care if he died or didn't come back. My heart was cold and bitter. He eventually came out of the water and called mom to tell her I tried to drown him. He went back to New Jersey on a train a few days later.

The second incident that sticks out to me is a time when Mike and I were out drinking and came home late. Stacey was waiting with a 2 × 4 in hand and screaming at me about how tired she was of me going out and doing whatever I wanted to do, while she stayed home with our daughter, Danielle. I got arrogant and looked her in the eyes and asked, "What are you going to do with that?" I took the beer bottle that was in my hand and smashed it over my own head, then she dropped the 2 × 4.

I don't know if the third incident was that same night or another night. Mike had a guy drop off crack cocaine at my house, and I didn't like that guy coming around. I told Mike about it and began to beat on him because I didn't think he was respecting me and what I wanted. He eventually left the house. He never hit me back! He wouldn't hit me because he loved me. Now I see that, then I was sure he was a coward. Stacey went to see if he was ok, and Mike told her to leave me before I killed her. He left and went back to NJ on a train.

When I got the call from my brother Mike saying that my dad had taken a tumble down the steps, I was in the middle of another relapse, if you want to call it that. My bouts of sobriety were always fleeting. I was smoking crack when I got the call, and it took three days to put the pipe down before getting on a plane to go see my dad. I remember going into the bathroom crying, while hitting the pipe and telling my girlfriend my dad was dead. At that point he still had a beating heart and was in the hospital, but I knew in my heart he was gone. I made it to New Jersey before he died. During one of my visits to see him in the hospital, he wasn't all that responsive. I saw that he had what they call "involuntary movements," where his arm would move up and down occasionally as if he were reaching out to someone, but he wasn't there. I had emotionally cut myself off from the situation so much so that as my mother sat by the bedside of the love of her life—the only man she loved, her husband, the father of her children, and my dad—I tapped her on the shoulder and whispered in her ear, "You know you got to get this over with and pull the plug. He doesn't want to be this way. I gotta go!"

I left the hospital and walked through a neighborhood that wasn't going to let me leave unbattered, much less high. I walked back before I bought any drugs or got killed, waited for my mom and Mike, and then we drove back to Delair. That moment still haunts me at times today. My dad died in a hospital a few days later. I never thought that's where he would die though. I thought it would be in a car accident, at home, or on the job, but not in the hospital. I was so disappointed in myself for how I turned out in his eyes. Again, it was all about me! I know the truth though. The person created became the person I was then, as a born-again Christian, created new. I am the person I am, not the person you say I am, not the person I say I am, but the person God says I am!

My daughter and I had a very strained relationship, or lack thereof, because of me. Most of it was like my own relationship with my dad. I was trying to be more of a friend than a father; I thought it would help her to talk to me better. Well, I did talk with her or maybe "at her." When she was very little, I did what dads do when they're around, I played games with her, read to her, sang to her at bedtime, and gave her baths. I allowed her to dress me up and do my hair and put make-up on me. We played Pretty Little Princess, Candyland, Chutes and Ladders, Boggle, and Hungry Hungry Hippos. We also climbed trees together and I often lit fires in the yard at night and would play with gasoline, lighting my body parts on fire without getting hurt. I would blow things up, you know, dad stuff. It was all fun until I needed to drink more than play. Showing my daughter that I could not be hurt was important to me. She needed to know nothing scared me, nothing could hurt me, and nothing would intimidate me. I tried to show her how fearless I was, that I had confidence in myself, and that I was a little crazy too, which would help when boys began coming around. I'm sure none of it worked the way I had hoped. That was all very wrong and is not how a father should be. As you'll read later, she has her own perspective on all this.

When she began getting into sports more, volleyball really started to take a hold of her. I was all about it because I played in high school, after hours occasionally, and sometimes at the beach in Wildwood, New Jersey. We practiced a lot, from what I remember. We would often practice wherever we were, even if it was just hitting the ball back and forth trying to work our way through the alphabet. In the back yard we put up a net and practiced back there also, spiking, setting, bumping, digs, you name it. We tried everything she was learning at practice.

I went to most of her extracurricular activities. I was at All-Pro Dads dinners and dances, too, when she was little. Not sober, so not there mentally, but I was physically there. That's something I didn't get at the time either. Being intoxicated divides the connection to others around you. Although you're there in body, you're not there in any other sense of the word, especially not as a father. I have memories of her that make me cry today. I wanted to be better for her, and I just couldn't get it. The weight of not being a good dad, the father she needed to have, was the heaviest of all the shame and guilt I carried.

The war was waging, and the devil was cunning. I had heard some things about Jesus, been to some churches that Stacey had dragged me to. and was introduced to being saved or becoming a born-again believer. Stacey prayed, probably a lot more than I noticed, but when I did notice I got on her about it, especially if I was drunk. Then I got nasty about it. One time, while using crack, I was in the bathroom and looking into the mirror at my reflection. I noticed something on my face that wasn't there before. At the top of my forehead right at the hairline, was a cross slightly raised up under my skin on the left side of my head. Then I noticed a slightly raised round bump on the right side of my head directly across from the cross. Not kidding! I was seeing this and didn't believe what I was seeing. I got Stacey and asked her if she saw anything on my forehead and she told me exactly what I was seeing! She told me it was a sign of the battle for my soul, and it was showing me I needed to choose either God or the devil. I was blown away but also had drugs to use. I didn't make any kind of decision at that point, shrugged it off, and tried not to look at it anymore. It lasted for a couple days, but we didn't talk about it after that. We didn't try to show anyone else either; why, I don't know. But it happened!

Stacey and I were at each other most days because of differences in behavior and thinking. My drinking was way out of control, and I was violent and abusive most days. We tried to do normal things like game nights with our daughter, have friends come over for small parties, go to dinner and the movies, but it was always interrupted by my drinking or drug use. I loved Stacey, and I wanted to be kind to her, do things for her, and show her how important she was to me. I just didn't do it well. I tried cooking breakfast for her in bed, buying her jewelry, flowers, and candy, and making a spectacle of Valentine's Day so it wasn't called "Doom's Day." I wanted to be with her, and I wanted us to be a family. I had a great example of what it should be like and look like growing up, but I couldn't seem to get it right or make it happen.

Skipping ahead a little, in 2010, I was thirty-six years old. I had been in construction since my teens and was barely holding onto a job for dear life as a sprinkler fitter, while living as a bachelor in Clearwater with a coworker and friend. I owned nothing but the clothes on my back and a bucket of hand tools. My license had been suspended since 2006 for two DUIs and three DWLS (driving while license suspended) with knowledge, and I hadn't done anything to try to get it reinstated. The company I was working for would release a truck to my coworker and I because he was the only one supposed to be driving it, since his license was good. So, the truck was in his name, but since I was the foreman, it was said to be released as my truck, and we were a team.

To set the stage, I had recently walked out on Stacey and Danielle, who was just turning ten. We had been in a relationship since 1996. After much consideration, I decided I wasn't helping things by being as reckless as I had been with them. Danielle was now old enough to see all the drug abuse and alcoholism in my life, and Stacey really needed a shot at getting her life back on track. I needed a life without family responsibilities because I couldn't live that kind of life very well. I wanted the party more than I wanted the family. It's sad to tell the truth but that was the truth. I had failed in so many aspects of life—trying to be a father, a good son, a decent individual, a kind, responsible worker, a good boyfriend/friend. I was not good at any of it.

I had planned on leaving Stacey, but never talked with her about it. One day after work, I set it up with Billy to move out and move in with him. When Stacey got home from work, I had all my bags packed and positioned at the front door. I asked her and Danielle to sit on the couch. I told Stacey I didn't love her any longer, and I was leaving. I asked Danielle if I could still be in her life, and she agreed. It was heart wrenching and not what I wanted, but I figured this was the best I could do to allow them a chance at a better life.

I was abusive to everyone in every way you can be abusive to another human being. I hit people I cared about, both male and female, verbally abused just about everyone, and mentally and emotionally abused those I loved to keep them at a distance and controlled. I did not commit any sexual abuse to others, though I had the thoughts. I was devious in allowing myself to be vulnerable so someone else would also. Then I would use what was told to me or what someone allowed me to be part of, to hurt, manipulate, and abuse the person. That is who I'd become after a life lived only to please myself. The use and abuse of drugs and alcohol only amplified who I was. It also helped carry me through the shame, blame, uselessness, and worthlessness I felt as a person who could not change. I couldn't forgive myself for who I had become. I now know I was never able to forgive myself anyways. I'm not saying this so you can agree with me. I'm stating a fact about all of us. You will never be able to forgive yourself either. Not for anything you've done. It's not our job to forgive ourselves! There would be no need for the judicial system if we were able to and no need for a Savior.

I had used crack as often as possible since I turned twenty. I pawned everything I could to get money, and I stole what I could to sell for money to buy more crack. I was using company gas cards to fill the drug dealer's gas tanks. I continued drinking every day until I was so wiped out, I couldn't function anymore, and my body couldn't operate without rest. I was depleting myself of all fuel. During that time, I saw my daughter on the weekends, and occasionally I would get together with Stacey. I also met a woman named Tammy, who lived in the same building as my buddy and me. We came to like one another, and we thought about getting together, but it just didn't seem to work in that sense. Friends is where it had to be.

The attraction on my end was fleeting, but Tammy would be an instrument of God, used to bring me closer to Him, although maybe that was not her intent. God is in control over all. Tammy was the first person to explain to me how special I was to God, believe it or not! She never shared the gospel though. You got to hear me on this… we were snorting cocaine together at about 3:00 a.m. on a Saturday, and she asks me, or tells me the following, "You have no idea how much God loves you, do you, Joe?"

I was like, "What?" We had never spoken about God before.

She then began to say things about how I had lived my life that no one could have known about unless they had been with me or were inside my head. She asked, "How do you think that you can just walk into these areas that most people don't walk out of, have drug dealers give you money back, and you walk away untouched and unharmed?" Now, that did happen, fifteen years prior, and I had never spoken about it to anyone. Plus, she didn't know me or anyone from New Jersey that I knew. How would she know to say that? She told me that God had a plan for me, and He was going to use me to help people. She told me there was a gold robe wrapped around me, and that she never felt so safe around "one" like me and that she had never met "one" like me. I didn't know what that meant, but she said it. "Yeah right! You going to finish that line, or should I?" That's what I said to her. This conversation ended with her telling me I need to stop using drugs. Do ya think?

Another time, I was eating magic mushrooms, and I heard her voice in my head. We had a conversation, and her lips never moved and neither did mine. I asked her the next day if that happened, and she agreed it did. It was and is hard to grasp. Weeks after that we walked a few blocks away from where we were staying to go fishing at a pier, and I noticed a girl fishing by herself. I thought I saw in her chest (i.e, inside her body) a black mass. It was like a blob of blackness inside her and it wasn't good. Then, when I turned my head the other way, there was a guy by himself, and I saw in his chest a white mass. Goodness is the only real way to describe it! So that meant to me that the black mass must have meant the girl was "bad."

I walked over to the guy and quickly engaged him in a conversation about drugs and recovery stuff.

Turned out he was coming off heroin and needed help. I talked him into coming back to my place, and I would take him to detox in the morning if he thought he could make it. Once he agreed, Tammy asked me "Do you think he's okay to stay with me tonight?"

I was like, "Why would you be asking me, you barely know me, and I don't know this guy!"

She said, "Yeah I know all that, but I know you know if he's ok or not to stay with me, so what's your answer?"

I told her, "Yes, he's ok." Well, I got him into detox. He was very thankful and said I was a godsend! Imagine that, after all I'd heard and what Tammy was telling me weeks prior, here I was helping someone I didn't even know. Following the twelfth step? You bet!

That moment stuck with me. Nothing really changed after that in my behavior or attitude, except I now had some pertinent information, if it were true. What Tammy told me, or what I heard her say was, "I'm invincible and I can't die because God won't allow it!" That's how I took that information, I'm not kidding, and boy, I ran with it. I picked up my ex one night to tell her all the amazing things I had just learned. I told her what Tammy had told me and explained that was why I hadn't died yet, and it was why I could use all the drugs I wanted and outlive most people who did the things I did, and I even tried to prove it to her. I picked her up in a company truck and drove to a road I knew had no streetlights. I turned the lights out on the truck while driving on the road to prove to her that even if anything happened, I wouldn't die. I was not even thinking that it didn't apply to her if it were true. She was freaking out and screaming for me to turn the lights back on. But I really believed God was going to maneuver the truck or drive the truck for me supernaturally. She was scared to say the least, but I didn't go far before turning them back on and getting us to our destination safely.

I continued to tell her how I got to that mindset. She wasn't sure what to say, and it wouldn't have made much difference whatever she had to say. I did what I wanted, when I wanted, where I wanted, all the time, and that was that.

Chapter 3
Strength

"Now the one who has fashioned us for this very purpose is God, who has given us the Spirit as a deposit, guaranteeing what is to come. (2 Corinthians 5:5)

Now you've gotten a small look at some of the moments that brought me to my October 28 arrest with my daughter in the back of my truck. If you recall, it was shame and worthlessness that was waying me down at that point. I was in jail again, and it was 2012. I could have killed my daughter, and I was done! It was so close to Halloween, of all days, which was my brother Chuck's birthday; ironic somehow, right? Jesus has a plan!

I laid there in general population, C100 level of the Pasco County Detention Center, FL. It was the third day after being arrested, waiting for them to call our row to come get razors to shave with, and I was going to get that razor and break it so I could use the razor blade to slit my throat. I figured I'd bleed out and end my useless life finally. As I laid there waiting, I felt something tear away, be removed, or step out from my body like I was unplugged or woken up. It was unbelievable! I looked around to see if anyone had witnessed what had happened, or if someone shook my bunk, but no one was paying attention to me! My next thought was, "Was that You (God)?" Before an answer would come, I fell asleep like a baby and never heard them call our row for razors. This, mind you, was early evening, maybe 4:30 or 5:00 p.m.

The next thing I heard was a pounding on the metal table in the pod and the CO yelling, "CHOW!" It was morning and breakfast time (4:30 a.m.), and even before my eyes opened or a thought came into my head, I heard a still, small voice, so calm, so clear, so pertinent, say, "Now, thank Jesus for saving your life." I began to sob immediately and rolled to my knees thinking, "God, you're real, and You love me?" Then I did it, I raised my hands to God and said it: "Thank you, Jesus, for saving my life!" I just knew He did. I felt a calming peace cover me like I had never experienced before. All the uselessness, worthlessness, shame, and guilt were gone. For the first time ever in my life, I knew how much worth I had, how useful I was, and that it all came from God. I was worth more than gold, and I had hope for a future. Jesus was real! I knew and acknowledged it right then and there. I was wrong and unworthy of being loved by Him, but He loved me anyway. At that moment, I was changed in ways yet to be revealed. That was the beginning. It was the end of "self" as I had chased it, but the beginning of a new Joe, a new life, a real life. I had become a new creation! I was saved. I had been reborn but didn't know it yet.

Another inmate told me about Celebrate Recovery a few days later, because I had a new hunger to read the Bible, and I could understand what I was reading that time around. He saw me and said I should go because he saw me go to AA, but Celebrate Recovery was the best of both AA and Christianity. I thought, *Sweet, I'll go*. I met a guy there named Ron, who was carrying the message of Christ in recovery. I liked what he had to say and after going a couple of times, I asked if I could have his number. I was getting bailed out and I wanted to see if he would be able to help me. He said he couldn't do that, but if I was serious about getting sober, I could meet him at Calvary Chapel in New Port Richie at Celebrate Recovery on a Saturday night at 6:00 p.m. and he'd give me his number. I told him, "I'll be there!"

I called my ex from the jail at some point, and she accepted the call. I told her that my mom was bailing me out, even though I asked her not to. I told her something had happened to me, and I wanted to know if I could at least come back to the house until I was sentenced. She hesitantly agreed, only so I could spend time with Danielle before going to prison. She didn't believe anything would be different, and neither one of us thought what was about to happen would ever happen. You might be thinking, what happened? Oh Lord, help me get all the things included here.

Chapter 4
Willingness

"For it is God who works in you, both to will and to work according to His good pleasure." (Phillipians 2:13 ESV)

Here are some of the things Jesus did with us within the first ten years.

He continues to do for us what we could never do for ourselves!

Here's what Jesus has done for Stacey and I.

1. Forgave us for all we have done or ever will do.
2. Saved us from death.
3. Changed us. We have been born again.
4. Brought us to the saving knowledge of who He is:

God the Father (YHWH), God the Son (Jesus), God the Holy Spirit (The Helper)

5. Changed our hearts and thinking.
6. Removed twenty-four years of alcoholism and a fifteen-year addiction to crack and other drugs.
7. Restored and reunited our family as an "intact family."
8. Trusted me to start a handyman business.
9. Helped me get a job at Home Depot with eight felonies on my record.
10. After seventeen years of being with Stacey and leaving her and Danielle in 2010, He brought us back together in 2012 and married us in 2013.
11. Helped me to get through one year of community control and four years of felony probation.
12. Paid $13,000.00 in court costs and fines, with $3,000.00 being paid anonymously.
13. Stacey graduated from college in her forties and became a state-certified radiologic technologist.

14. In 2016, with not $100 in the bank, He helped me purchase a company truck that we own today, as well as another one.
15. I needed to have a breathalyzer installed in the truck for two years, and it's been out since February of 2018
16. I had not had a license since 2006, but today I have a valid driver's license.
17. . Is restoring the relationship with Danielle I thought would be lost.
18. Has made moments possible for me to make amends for the harm I've done to others.
19. Uses our testimony to touch countless lives.
20. Told us to pray over our dog Tinker and He would heal her cancer. The cancer was removed.
21. Healed many scars from past hurts, habits, and hang-ups.
22. Allowed Stacey and me to take a honeymoon cruise.
23. Healed my heart from an abortion I was part of, and I was able to pray with the mother of our unborn child.
24. Allowed me to become a state-certified residential contractor in the state of Florida.

25. Allows me to help alcoholics and drug addicts like I once was.
26. Allowed us to own our home.
27. Is training us to be leaders in the recovery community.
28. We serve in our church.
29. Healed relationship wounds not able to be rectified by human ability or counseling.
30. Is removing my lustful desires for pornography.
31. Is allowing us to be grandparents to our granddaughter.
32. June 19, 2023: my brother, Mike, got saved at age fifty-seven, and Jesus used me to help shine His light into my brother's life.

These are just some of the highlights. The work of Jesus for all of us is insurmountable and unthinkable. There are no words to describe how vast the Father's love is for us!

If He can do this for us, you know He can do anything!

When I got saved in jail while I was on my bunk and ready to kill myself, everything changed, and things immediately began to happen. God started to reveal Himself and His power. I heard His voice very clear and still do. Now, this voice is unexplainable as far as tone, sound, and type; it's more of a knowledge of His voice. It comes from within but can be heard with my ears at times, although I don't believe anyone else hears it when I do. That said, I'm going to tell you some stuff here, and it's going to sound crazy, unbelievable, and supernatural. It is all that, and believe me, if it didn't happen to me, I wouldn't believe it either. So here we go.

I jumped from my bunk that morning after sobbing and listening to God tell me Jesus is real. I gathered myself, made it into the chow line, and got my tray. *Now, hear all this, Jesus please open the ears and eyes of those reading this, Amen.* I sat down with my tray and began to eat. As I chewed, it felt as though the food was multiplying after every bite, like it was growing larger in my mouth. I was noticing it but quickly writing it off as my mind playing tricks on me. Then, as I took another fork full, I noticed the food wasn't shrinking on my plate. Yeah, you heard me right, it wasn't disappearing as I was eating, and I was getting full. I stood up to take the tray to the trash can, and God spoke once again and said, "Now give it to someone else!" I walked by an inmate sitting on his bunk who I believed lost a bet and had to pay with his breakfast tray. So, I said, "You want this?" He said, "You sure?" and I replied, "Yep." And that was it. I didn't go into any big explanation because truly I thought I was losing my mind. I was hearing voices, food was not disappearing as I ate it, and I didn't know what was happening, but I had peace in my heart at the same time. My mind was so confused, but somehow, I was okay with everything that was happening.

I had been in C100 for three days, and I had found a Bible to read, because that's what I usually gravitated to when I was in jail. Yeah, I get "jailhouse religion," but when I began to read that time, it was different, and I understood it differently than before. There was a big black guy in the dorm, and one day he took notice of me. He came over to the table where I was sitting and reading and sat down across from me and said,

"You new, right?"

Me: "Yeah."

Inmate: "No I mean to prayer."

Me: "What?"

Inmate: "You see that guy over there with the 666 tattooed on the back of his head. That's one you should not try to speak to alone! You, me, we ain't strong enough for that one!"

Oh Lord, what was going on here? Did that guy know that something just happened to me? Was it a set-up, or was it for real? Did I have a sign on my back that said, "Mess with me spiritually?" I couldn't seem to get it together. He continued and asked, "You don't know do you?" This was midmorning on the same day. He said, "Do you know what the letters B.I.B.L.E. stand for? I shook my head no. He said something like, "Oh man, I got a lot to tell you!" So, he shared with me the meaning of the letters and began to minister to me about different things and told me his story of being back in jail.

Turns out, it had been a mistake, and he was going home shortly, and it was all true. He told me God was going to use me in a mighty way to help people. Once again, another person I barely know telling me that God is going to us me to help people, just like Tammy said about a month or two prior to this happening. Then it all stopped. No more supernatural

Willingness

things happened, no more voices were heard, and that day came to an end. I went to sleep in anticipation of what was going to transpire next.

The next day, everything was normal, and I felt great. The rest of the time spent in C100 was fine, and I decided to collect call Stacey to see if I could come back to the house until I got sentenced, so I could spend time with Danielle and her as I said earlier. My heart was different, and I was regretting how I walked out on them two years before, so I told Stacey I knew Jesus now! She didn't believe me but agreed to come pick me up and allow me to stay with them until I went to prison. Well, when I got out and called her from the company cell phone (it was in my property bag; it still worked and had a charge), she came to get me.

On the ride back, Danielle, Stacey, and I were in the car and Stacey had brought me a carton of 305 Menthol cigarettes. I was hesitant but took them and lit up. Cigarettes stayed in my life a little longer than I wanted them to, but God had a plan. During the ride, I was telling them what happened to me: that I heard God's voice and Jesus was real. Stacey wasn't buying any of it, and my daughter surely wasn't either, but we got back to the house and began life again. I had the tasks of getting to recovery meetings, finding a job, and getting things in order before I went to prison. It was not going to be easy since I was an eight-time convicted felon with no valid driver's license, no money, no car, no clothes, and no tools, except one bucket of small hand tools. Where would I begin?

Well, I had two good feet, I was well rested, and not in bad shape, so walking was what I did. I walked everywhere for a while, and Stacey eventually asked me if I wanted a ride, and she began to help me. I'm sure it was against her better instincts. While I was waiting in limbo for court dates, I went to temp agencies, sought out work on Craigslist, and landed some odd jobs to earn some money. I bought a mountain bike and a bus pass. Stacey and I would talk about things: past things, new things, and what my plans were. We didn't sleep together or in the same room for two months. One day while talking and sitting in the bedroom together, she said to me, "You aren't the same person." (She doesn't remember saying this to me, but it happened.) I told her, "I tried to tell you that Jesus did something to me. I got saved!"

If you remember, I had to meet that guy from the jail, Ron, at Calvary Chapel Church on a Saturday night at 6:00 p.m. at Celebrate Recovery. If I were to remain sober and learn to walk the walk, I was ready and willing to do whatever it took to stick close to Jesus and far away from drugs and alcohol. So, I went there every Saturday until I saw Ron and finally shook his hand. I got his number and began a recovery relationship with him. I soon learned he had a mobile ministry going, not an organized ministry. You would get into his vehicle, and you would be bombarded with the gospel, everything Jesus, everything recovery, everything needed to point you in the right direction. He was humble, kind, courteous, called me out, listened, directed, encouraged, and shined as one of the biggest lights I ever saw. I gripped onto him for dear life. I wanted what he had, and I wanted to know Christ like he did! I saw how he truly cared for others and loved his wife and friends. I was so out of touch with people like Ron that I didn't really think they existed any longer.

I knew I had to speak with Tammy, Billy, Amanda, and my ex-boss to make things right. I reached out to all of them and explained my situation. My boss didn't file any charges. He just needed to get the company phone back and couldn't hire me back, of course. His hands were tied, and I wasn't trying to get my job back. I was ready for change; heck, I was in the middle of it. Tammy, Amanda, and Billy were still my friends and were there for me. Billy eventually moved to another apartment complex where he still is today. Tammy hired me to remodel her van and work at her daughter's house; even her daughter hired me to help with an RV that I didn't do a great job at. I mistakenly put battery cables on the wrong terminals. Nothing happened, thank God, but it was embarrassing. They moved away, and Tammy started to use her van to travel. She died a few years later when she got hit by a truck on a deserted road in Texas, or someplace like that. She was probably living out of the van I helped her with. Her daughter called me one night to tell me, and I cried. God rest her soul.

I got out of jail on November 15, 2012, and my sentencing took place on July 19, 2013. Within those seven months, I heard God daily, my life changed dramatically, the Holy Spirit ministered to me directly, the Bible came to life to me as I read it, supernaturally prayers were immediately answered, circumstances and situations worked out to my favor, and the people around me witnessed the power, majesty, and love that could only come from a relationship with Jesus, being born again and saved. I once lived a black-and-white type of life, but now things are in color. It wasn't because of what I was doing or that I deserved a break, because I didn't. I deserved nothing!

I gained a job as a ranch hand/handyman at a stable in Lutz, Florida. My pay eventually became $15.00 an hour after I had been making $10.00 an hour for almost a year. At the ranch, I prayed on my hands and knees, feeling gratitude like never before and watched, listened, and learned from the Holy Spirit. I began to see what obedience looked like when He would direct me to pray with and for animals. Once, a mini horse put her head against mine as I knelt before her to pray over her. It was amazing and unbelievable, as if she knew what was going on. I listened to the Spirit lead me in prayer as I cried out to God, so scared to be sentenced to prison, pleading for reasons why He shouldn't put me in prison, and then hearing, "You won't be going to prison."

I was packing up at work one day a little early, I'd say twenty-five minutes early, and the Holy Spirit said to me, "You're being paid to a certain time." I packed up the blower and stopped working because my pride told me, *I did a good enough job, and they aren't paying me enough anyways. I did what they are paying for. I'm done.* Then, I was instructed to unpack the blower and continue to work until He said I was done. I was no longer representing myself. I was now a representative of Him, and He was the boss. He tells me when it's good enough, when I'm done, and when I clock out, not anyone else. I thought this was crazy. Stacey was going to come to pick me up and would have to wait until God said I was done. I remember Him saying, "She'll be here when she should be." I finished using the blower to clean off the driveway, packed everything up, and as I was doing it, Stacey came pulling into the driveway to get me, not a minute past when I should have been finished either. Perfect timing. God's timing is always perfect!

Chapter 5
Honesty

"Whoever speaks the truth, gives honest evidence, but a false witness utters deceit" (Proveerbs 12:17 ESV)

One afternoon while I was out in one of the pastures cleaning brush and mowing, I started thinking about the voice I was hearing and wondering if it was just my subconscious, like my mom would tell me about as a kid. She would say, "There's two voices you're going to hear: one is the devils, and one is God's. The one that tells you to do good things is God and the one that tells you to do bad things is the devil." Is that what was going on? Was I just conjuring up that old story from my mom that now was manifesting its way through my memories into my life? Was it just my subconscious? Was it God's voice? As this was all swirling around in my head, I heard the voice say very loudly, "Drop the sticks and call Sober Solutions." I had been calling that place for almost two weeks, but no one ever picked up when I called. I left messages but didn't get any return calls. I didn't do what the voice told me to do.

Sober Solutions was an outpatient rehabilitation facility, and I had been trying to get in there before I went to court so it looked like I was doing what I was supposed to do before I went in front of the judge. There I was again, hearing the voice, the same voice from jail, the same voice in prayer, the same voice just the other day that told me He's my boss. Then He got louder, and He said, "I said, drop the sticks and call Sober Solutions now!" So, I did and to my amazement after two rings I heard, "Hello, Sober Solutions can I help you?" I didn't say a word because I was in shock and stunned. Then the voice on the other end says again, "Hello?" I snapped to and said, "I'm sorry, hello, I wasn't expecting anyone to answer, but anyway I need to speak to someone about getting started there." The man on the other end of the line said, "Well, I don't work here, but I just happened to be sitting near the phone when it rang. Hold on I'll get someone for you." When I was put on hold, I was in shock. I didn't believe what was going on, but this time it saturated my entire being and I knew in my heart of hearts I was hearing

God Himself. I got set up with Sober Solutions and began treatment the following week.

There was a Sunday morning, we were on our way to Lakeview Community Church for service, and we stopped at 7-11 to get coffee and gas. Stacey and I both got into the store and God said, "I want you to turn to Stacey and tell her that the day in the rehab, when you two locked eyes with each other, I was using her at a time when she felt useless to get to you." So, I turned to Stacey right there in the middle of the store. With tears in my eyes, I told her what God had just told me. She got emotional and said, "I have to show you something." When we walked outside and got back into the car, she handed me her cell phone and said, "This is a text I got this morning from a woman I know at the class I'm taking to become a life coach. The following is the actual text message format.

> "The spirit put this on my heart to text you… when you mentioned you didn't have the burning bush experience, that is called deliverance grace. Your experience is called sustainable grace, God parted the sea with deliverance grace but used sustainable grace to keep them the forty years. With

> that said, God used His sustainable grace in you throughout your life with your husband to bring him to deliverance grace. Just like the jailor in Acts 16:31 "you believed on the Lord Jesus Christ, and you were saved and your household. The spirit put it on my heart to tell you keep strong!"

I'm not making this stuff up, people. I was floored once again, and these things just kept on happening and still happen to this day.

Jesus married Stacey and me on July 7, 2013. After seventeen years of living in sin, being together against every suggestion of recovery and most people in our lives, and my jail time, we endured. My mom & dad were there when Stacey and I got married. Stacey had her mom and dad, who hadn't been in the same place together for about thirty years, and they finally spoke to one another. Our daughter was the DJ for the wedding, and my brothers in Christ were there. Ron was my best man, and it got done. During the ceremony, the usual words were spoken, no handmade vows were written, but the Chaplin who conducted our wedding, and who is a friend of mine, said these words:

"If anyone has any reason why these two should not be married, keep it to yourself." That was priceless! The wedding was supposed to happen years prior, and I called it off. Jesus puts all things right in place where they need to be, when they need to be. Stacey has been an instrument of God, showing His love to those in her family and me. If it weren't for Stacey deciding to go to church all those years ago and answering "the Call" for her life, this all may be a very different story. Thank you Stacey Lee Wood Seabolt for not letting the enemy steal your joy, rob you of your inheritance, and lead you astray. My beautiful, beautiful wife, thank you! Besides Jesus, you are *the* most special person in my life today!

Now I'm going to tell you about the court hearing that took place on July 19, 2013. They had no idea I had already been informed of the verdict!

"Pasco County Court, State vs Joseph Alan Seabolt. Is Joseph in the courtroom? Please come forward to the podium." The following is the actual court stenographer's notes from my court case in 2013.

APPEARANCES

APPEARING ON BEHALF OF
THE STATE OF FLORIDA:

Vincent Petty, Assistant State Attorney
Office of Bernie McCabe, State Attorney
Sixth Judicial Circuit, Pasco County
7530 Little Road
New Port Richey, Fl 34654

APPEARING ON BEHALF OF
THE DEFENDANT JOSEPH SEABOLT:

Shahtia Gay-Hairston, Assistant Public Defender
Office of Bob Dillinger, Public Defender
Sixth Judicial Circuit, Pasco County
7530 Little Road
New Port Richey, Fl 34654

THE COURT: I thought it came from you.

MS. GAY-HAIRSTON: Oh. And, Your Honor, in addition to that our office had him screened by Phoenix House and he does appear --

THE COURT: By what?

MS. GAY-HAIRSTON: Phoenix House.

THE COURT: Oh, Phoenix House.

MS. GAY-HAIRSTON: He would be able to go to Phoenix House if you thought that inpatient treatment was necessary. He wants to go to Phoenix house, Your Honor.

The only issue is, from what I know, that even if you decide to not send him to prison and you want to do Phoenix House, from what I know so far he would have to be remanded in the jail today and that's the quickest way for him to get a bed.

THE COURT: Right.

MS. GAY-HAIRSTON: They don't have one available right at the moment.

And, Your Honor, other than that we just want to have three people briefly speak for him. It will be under two minutes each.

First, I would like his sponsor to come up. His name is Mr. Nohr, Ronald Nohr, Your Honor.

THE COURT: Good morning, sir.

(Witness sworn.)

THE COURT: Would you state your name.

MR. NOHR: My name is Ronald Nohr.

THE COURT: Mr. Nohr, what would you like me to know about Mr. Seabolt?

MR. NOHR: Well, Your Honor, I met Mr. Seabolt about eight months ago in the Land O' Lakes Detention. I've been in recovery circles for about 28 years.

THE COURT: You were visiting, I take it?

MR. NOHR: Actually, I'm a volunteer. I've been volunteering --

THE COURT: Right. I meant you weren't in custody.

MR. NOHR: No.

THE COURT: Okay.

MR. NOHR: Yeah. I carry a message of recovery, and in the '90s it was Zephyrhills for about six years and then for the past seven years it's been Land O' Lakes.

I myself, like I said, I've been in recovery for about 28 years. I'm retired law enforcement from out of state, retired in '94 as a third grade detective.

I've been in the trenches of recovery as far

Honesty

as, you know, trying to make a difference. You know as well as I do, the recurrence and the relapse rate is staggering as far as alcoholism or drug addiction, but I do continue to stand in the trenches.

I've never stood before a magistrate on behalf of a sponsee. This is the first time in 28 years I've done it. As I said, I met Mr. Seabolt about eight months ago.

I met him while inside, and it's been a policy, and I respect the rules and the regs, that no personal information would be passed while in the vicinity.

My attitude is this is where I am, this is where you can find me when you come out. You know, look me up. And that's what happens. They come to a meeting, see me at a meeting, and the process begins.

I require three musts, call me every day for 30 days, don't lie to me, and call me before you pick up a drink or a drug. And that's been again my musts and I don't deviate from that, that's my boundaries.

Joe has been -- he's adhered to those requests and my boundaries for these past eight months. I personally heard his inventory. I'm not an ordained minister. You know, I just profess to be a godly man doing what I think is right.

I've heard his personal inventory. He's married his beloved sweetheart just two weeks ago. He asked me to be his best man, which was an honor in and of itself.

I would just say that, you know, Joe has shown me promise. He's shown me that he's equipped with the tools to press on and to be a law-abiding citizen in this community.

I appeal to the justice system, I appeal to the mercy of this Court, Judge, and certainly your justice.

THE COURT: Are you familiar with his attendance at AA?

MR. NOHR: Well, I can tell you this, I speak to Joe at least every other day; he goes to at least four meetings a week, two of which I personally pick him up and take him to these meetings.

And I stood up for him to be a leader at a Saturday night meeting at a location. I sponsor him for that position and that's pending to carry the message of hope and strength and recovery.

Honesty

1 THE COURT: Thank you, sir.
2 MS. GAY-HAIRSTON: Your Honor, next I would
3 like to call Jimmy Shibal. I said his name wrong,
4 Your Honor.
5 MR. SHIBLEY: That's okay.
6 THE COURT: Sir, do you swear or affirm to
7 tell the truth?
8 MR. SHIBLEY: I do.
9 (Witness sworn.)
10 THE COURT: Would you state your name for the
11 record.
12 MR. SHIBLEY: My name is James Shibley.
13 I met Joe a few months -- well, a few months
14 back. I attend Celebrate Recovery, and I, through
15 God's grace and mercy, have been sober now for
16 seven years.
17 I met Mr. Seabolt, and he attends our Saturday
18 night -- or our Wednesday night family Bible group.
19 And it's just a group of individual people from
20 different churches and all and we study the Lord's
21 word.
22 And I've seen great strides that Joe has
23 taken. And just for the short amount of time that
24 I've known him, Your Honor, that he's -- I do see a
25 godly man working in him. And he will -- he is

```
 1      becoming a productive citizen and doing his best.
 2           We all have stumbles, but, you know, that's
 3      why we're all together and that's why we all
 4      support one another.
 5           THE COURT: All right. Thank you, sir.
 6           MR. SHIBLEY: Thank you.
 7           MS. GAY-HAIRSTON: And lastly, Your Honor, I'd
 8      ask that his wife, Stacy, if she could come and
 9      speak.
10           THE COURT: Good morning, Miss. Do you swear
11      firm to tell the truth?
12           MS. SEABOLT: Yes, I do.
13 (Witness sworn.)
14           THE COURT: Would you state your name.
15           MS. SEABOLT: Stacy Lee Seabolt now.
16           THE COURT: What would you like me to know?
17           MS. SEABOLT: Well, I've been with Joe for the
18      last 17 and a half years, through a lot of good and
19      bad times, and I've seen and been with him through
20      --
21           THE COURT: That is a long engagement.
22           MS. SEABOLT: Yes. Very well.
23           THE COURT: Maybe a record. Go ahead.
24           MS. SEABOLT: And I've seen, you know, many,
25      many attempts at getting sober and this time
```

there's been a great change in him that only God could have done, and this time he's committed and devoted and wants to reach out and give back and that's what he does.

He started his own business and he carries the message through that and --

THE COURT: What business is that?

MS. SEABOLT: He started a handyman business. And he -- you know, I drive him to a lot of meetings, and he just started going in and taking meetings to the detox at the Harbor.

THE COURT: How does he get to his jobs?

MS. SEABOLT: Either bus, bicycle, or I do.

THE COURT: He doesn't drive?

MS. SEABOLT: No, not at all. And, you know, he goes to meetings.

THE COURT: Are you employed?

MS. SEABOLT: I am.

THE COURT: What is your employment?

MS. SEABOLT: I work at a daycare center at night.

THE COURT: What do you mean at night?

MS. SEABOLT: We're open until 10:00 at night.

THE COURT: I see. So what are your physical hours?

1   MS. SEABOLT: 3:00 to 10:00. Or -- and lately
2   it's been -- I've been leaving at like 8:00. I've
3   been working 3:00 to 8:00 to, you know, go to
4   meetings and like --
5   THE COURT: Like Al-Anon, you mean?
6   MS. SEABOLT: I go to Celebrate Recovery also
7   now.
8   THE COURT: Are you a recovering alcoholic as
9   well?
10   MS. SEABOLT: Yes. And so we go to Celebrate
11   Recovery. I go two nights a week, he goes three.
12   We attend Bible study on Wednesday night. We're in
13   church every Sunday.
14   And like it was just stated, you know, we just
15   got married on the 7th, and I just see like amazing
16   change that's been taking place over the last nine
17   months.
18   THE COURT: All right. Thank you, Miss.
19   MS. GAY-HAIRSTON: Your Honor, lastly,
20   Mr. Seabolt would like to address the Court.
21   Your Honor, before he addresses the Court, I
22   just want to say that he stands before you today --
23   THE COURT: He's what?
24   MS. GAY-HAIRSTON: He stands before you today.
25   He's really at peace, Your Honor. I mean whatever

you decide, he's leaving it in your hands, but he's really at peace. He really has -- he has the peace of God with him.

And I mean if you decide prison, if you decide not prison, he is really at peace with whatever decision you make and he wanted to make sure the Court knew that as well.

THE COURT: Before he speaks, let me ask Mr. Billings, where does he score? Or, I'm sorry, Mr. --

MR. PETTY: Mr. Petty, Judge.

THE COURT: Pennington?

MR. PETTY: He scores DOC eligible at 33.5 points.

MS. GAY-HAIRSTON: 33.5 points.

THE COURT: Okay. So supervision would be a lawful sentence?

MR. PETTY: Yes, it would, Judge.

THE COURT: Not desirable --

MR. PETTY: No.

THE COURT: -- in the mind of the State, but lawful?

MR. PETTY: Correct, Judge.

THE COURT: Let me hear from the State next before I hear from the defendant.

MR. PETTY: Judge, he does not have a history of successful probation.

THE COURT: Quite the contrary.

MR. PETTY: Quite the contrary, yes.

In 1998 we cut him a very large break. He was given a YO on an aggravated battery. Less than a year after he was placed on that YO supervision, he violated, cocaine and paraphernalia. He then served community control probation after that.

He does not have a successful probation history. He had a DUI in 1998. Then after that we've got the '04 DWLSR, '04 DWLSR. He's got a consistent history of disregarding the law with his license.

2006 he picked up the second DUI in Pasco for which he did not successfully complete probation, he VOPed.

THE COURT: I'm sorry. When?

MR. PETTY: 2006. He VOPed and was given a county sentence on that. Then in 2008 he picked up yet another DWLSR. He's continuing to drive while he was habitual and while he was on a DUI suspension that he never reinstated.

This case isn't the run-of-the-mill DUI. He wasn't stopped for just swerving or weaving. He

Honesty

was stopped for driving at an extremely high rate of speed while he had two young children ages 13 and 14 in the rear of his truck that the deputy was extremely concerned.

THE COURT: His children?

MR. PETTY: I do not recall if they were his children or not, Judge.

THE COURT: I think they were.

MR. PETTY: But they were driving at a very high rate of speed with those two children in the back causing them great danger and causing the officer to be very concerned and pulled him over, at which point he was not cooperative and would not provide a breaths sample here.

The State's offer has always been prison. We would ask -- the offer has been 13 months for the last several pretrials. We'd want no less than 13 months here for him based upon all the facts and circumstances.

This is his third DUI within a ten-year period. Unsuccessful history of probation. He continues to blatantly disregard the HTO and the suspensions on his license due to the numerous DWLSRs. We feel that prison would be appropriate, Judge.

```
 1        THE COURT:  Could you refresh my recollection
 2   as to if there are any mandatory provisions of
 3   the -- is this a third DUI or a fourth DUI?
 4        MR. PETTY:  It's a third within 10 DUI, Judge.
 5        The mandatory provisions would be 30 days
 6   county, would be a mandatory adjudication.
 7        THE COURT:  Wait, wait.  Slow down, please.
 8        MR. PETTY:  Adjudicate.  The fine range would
 9   be, because it is the child enhancements, it would
10   be between 4- and $5,000.  The DL revocation is ten
11   years.  There is a 90-day impound.
12        THE COURT:  Wait, wait, wait.  Ten years DL?
13        MR. PETTY:  Yes.
14        THE COURT:  90-day impound?
15        MR. PETTY:  And the multiple offender DUI
16   school and any recommended treatment.  One session
17   of the victim impact panel, and we'd like to make
18   sure that that is a live attendance and not an
19   Internet course.  No alcohol, bars or clubs.  Not a
20   condition --
21        THE COURT:  Let me ask you this, Counsel:  Are
22   you aware of anything that shows the victim impact
23   has any impact?
24        MR. PETTY:  Yes, Judge.
25        THE COURT:  Because all of the research in
```

1 this field shows that it has zero impact.
2   MR. PETTY: Judge, the individual --
3   THE COURT: Not necessarily as to victim
4 impact, but as to what affect these types of
5 programs have on individuals, because they always
6 think it's somebody else, it's not them.
7   MR. PETTY: I speak monthly at these panels as
8 well as numerous victims of DUIs, and at the end of
9 the session I see a number of first time DUI
10 offender that actually do come up to us very
11 apologetic, extremely sincere, and I don't see
12 their names come back on any of my DUI invest
13 calendars. And all the misdemeanor calendars do
14 hit my desk. So I think the victim impact panels
15 here are being successful.
16   THE COURT: Let me rephrase it. Do you have
17 anything other than anecdotal information?
18   MR. PETTY: No, Judge. I have not seen --
19   THE COURT: That would be very helpful, I
20 think, to have.
21   MR. PETTY: I would agree, Judge.
22   THE COURT: So because my wife has always
23 asked me well, why did you do something, why did
24 you include something as a sentence, and I'll say
25 because it seemed right. And she'll say that's a

```
 1        pretty bad reason for doing something.
 2             MR. PETTY: Yes.
 3             THE COURT: Without any evidence based
 4        research to support it.
 5             MR. PETTY: Yeah. I don't know of any studies
 6        on it. I just know that based upon the chief judge
 7        in this circuit it's not only statutory, it is
 8        mandatory with all DUIs.
 9             THE COURT: Wow, I'm impressed by that.
10             MR. PETTY: Yes.
11             THE COURT: Okay. Go ahead.
12             MR. PETTY: And there's also not a condition
13        of probation, it would be a two-year interlock
14        device.
15             THE COURT: Okay. Go ahead.
16             MS. GAY-HAIRSTON: Your Honor, I don't think
17        you put him under oath yet.
18             THE COURT: Do you swear to tell the truth?
19             THE DEFENDANT: Yes, I do.
20   (Defendant sworn.)
21             THE COURT: State your name.
22             THE DEFENDANT: My name is Joseph Alan
23        Seabolt.
24             Your Honor, first of all, I apologize for
25        meeting you in these circumstances.
```

Honesty

As you've heard my history is not up to par.

THE COURT: It's awful.

THE DEFENDANT: Yes. And this last time I got arrested, while I was driving that was my daughter in the bed of the truck, and --

THE COURT: You must feel awful about that?

THE DEFENDANT: Yes. She could have been killed, and I know that now. At the time I didn't see it as that, and I didn't even think that those blue lights were for me when they went on at the time.

And when I was locked up and I went in the jail in my mind I knew that if I walked out of there I was going to continue to drink and drug and that I'd probably destroy that relationship with my daughter or have -- or maybe kill her. And I didn't want to do that and I was ready to slit my throat when those razors were going to come around, and this was on Halloween.

THE COURT: Last year?

THE DEFENDANT: And it was a miraculous change.

THE COURT: Last year?

THE DEFENDANT: Last year, yes. And there in jail there was a miraculous change and the only thing that I can tell you is that the Lord Jesus Christ came into my heart like something I've never felt before. I wasn't a believer in God or Jesus Christ.

And he took away any kind of condemnation, shame, blame, feelings that I didn't want to live anymore, and at that moment I knew that there was something different going on inside me.

And when I walked out of there and I met Ron Nohr in there, he was the first guy that I ever kept my word with and so I showed up at Celebrate Recovery, and I've been doing that ever since.

I do go to AA. AA is my foundation. I do take AA meetings into the Harbors now on Mondays at 10:00 AM. I pray every morning and I thank God every night for staying sober, because I do nothing to stay sober except go to these meetings and do the things that AA asks me to do.

And I definitely I'm looking into becoming an addictions counselor, that's my hopes and my dreams right now. And I leave this situation in your hands, and the Lord is standing with me and I feel peace for whatever judgment you may pass.

That's all I have to say, Your Honor.

THE COURT: Okay. Ms. Neesham, does Probation

Honesty

1 and Parole have the capacity to test for alcohol
2 amongst -- along with the six panel?
3 　　MS. NEESHAM: Your Honor, it's a --
4 　　THE COURT: A strip?
5 　　MS. NEESHAM: -- a breath stick.
6 　　THE COURT: All right.
7 　　MS. NEESHAM: It's positive or negative. If
8 it's positive, it will just lavish.
9 　　THE COURT: So it really covers about 12 hours
10 or six hours, something like that?
11 　　MS. NEESHAM: Well, if Your Honor wants a true
12 test done, you would have to order that it be sent
13 to lab each time.
14 　　THE COURT: Well, the great thing about
15 Mr. Seabolt is that, you know, he's not a quiet
16 drunk. You know, when he drinks he raises hell and
17 so I suppose he's going to be easily caught.
18 　　He's currently still going to Sober Solutions?
19 　　MS. GAY-HAIRSTON: Yes, he is, Your Honor.
20 　　THE COURT: Mr. Seabolt, this is quite rare
21 for me, I have to say this. In fact, it may be a
22 singular in many, many years, but I actually
23 believe you. So I'm going to take a chance on you.
24 　　I do adjudicate you guilty of both counts --
25 excuse me, both Informations, driving while license

suspended, felony habitual; as well as the DUI, third time DUI.

As to the DUI, I sentence you to the 30 days county jail, credit for time served. A $4,000 fine. Ten years DL suspension or revocation. Ninety-day impound. Multi-offender school to start it within 30 days of your release, successfully complete it the first time. Victim impact appearance live. Two years interlock.

And as to the DUI, that's 12-07570, I'm placing you on two years community control with drug offender conditions, followed by two and a half years probation, drug offender conditions.

As to the suspended -- excuse me. As to the suspended DL charge, 7566, I've already adjudicated you. I'm placing you on two years community control, followed by three years probation.

I'm going to favorably consider early rollover and early term after you successfully complete half as an incentive.

Special conditions of both supervisions are that you attend AA twice a week -- strike this. This is only a mandatory provision of the community control that you attend AA minimum of twice a week, that you submit to a screening once within every

Honesty

30-day time period, minimum six panel plus oxycodone plus alcohol.

That you successfully complete your substance abuse treatment that you begun the first time. No alcohol possessed, consumed or in your household. A curfew when you get on probation of 8:00 PM to 6:00 AM. The exception will be for work or directly to or from work.

And a special condition of both the community control and the probation is that further that you keep a -- excuse me. What is the term from AA in terms of this gentleman that spoke?

MS. GAY-HAIRSTON: Sponsor.

THE COURT: Sponsor. That you keep a sponsor.

Special condition is that you perform two speaking sessions per month where you speak as to your experience as to being an alcoholic and the damage that you've done.

One of them can be AA, but the other one has to be approved by your PO. It can be church, school, Victim Impact, but it has to be approved by the probation officer, and that will require monthly proof of having done that.

I'm not going to give you any more jail time beyond the mandatory 30 days. And so my observation is it looks like you've got 19 days in, so you may only have a couple of days before you're released by the Sheriff.

Now, I'm sure you've heard about my sentencing practices, most everybody has. I'm not going to give you a suspended sentence, because you should understand if you violate the terms of the supervision in a meaningful, substantial, intentional manner, you're not just looking at 18 months or a year and a half prison, you're looking at the full boat.

THE DEFENDANT: I understand, Your Honor.

THE COURT: All right. You do have 30 days to file a notice of appeal. If you can't afford counsel, counsel will be appointed for you. Do you understand?

THE DEFENDANT: Yes, I do.

THE COURT: Good luck to you.

THE DEFENDANT: Thank you, Your Honor.

MR. PETTY: The only additional thing, there's invest costs on the DUI of $104 and the DWLSR of $26, both to Pasco, Judge.

THE COURT: I'll order that as well as conditions of probation.

$200 attorney's fees, $50 appointment, $550 in

court costs, and $100 cost of prosecution.

And is it Mr. Pennington?

MR. PETTY: Petty, Judge.

THE COURT: Petty?

MR. PETTY: Yes.

THE COURT: P-E-T-T-Y.

MR. PETTY: Yes.

THE COURT: Mr. Petty, I certainly appreciate the State's position.

As you know I rarely deviate --

MR. PETTY: Yes, Judge.

THE COURT: -- from taking a very hard view of these matters, but I felt this was the right thing to do in this case.

MR. PETTY: I understand, Judge.

THE COURT: So thank you.

MR. PETTY: Certainly.

THE COURT: Okay.

(HEARING CONCLUDED.)

The proceeding picks up right after the state attorney and the judge are discussing the docket order and my public defender is trying to get my case going. As you saw in the transcript, the judge admittedly says he's known for being strict and not deviating from the state guidelines and everyone who went before him was sentenced to prison. In his own words, "I thought this was the right thing to do!" Not my will (thoughts/plans) Father, but Your will (thoughts/plans) be done! When I was in the inmate van riding back to the jail, it was quiet in there. I was not a favorite because no one understood how I wasn't going to prison, and neither could I. This is where it all really began.

I was placed on Community Control (CC) for twenty-four months followed by five years of felony probation, along with many other requirements included in the sentencing. While at Community Control, I had to find legal employment and pay monthly supervision fees, court costs, and fines totaling $13,000.00. So, I began submitting applications everywhere and as a felon it was not easy to land a decent job or any job, but I finally got a call from Home Depot. When I asked my Community Control officer if I could go to the interview, she smirked and said, "They aren't going to hire you, you'll be wasting your time," but she let me go. They wound up calling me back for a second interview, and she said the same thing but let me go to that interview also. They hired me and she was so angry; she thought I lied on my application.

There was a sheet I had to fill out every week. It had each day of the week and every hour of every day listed. I had to make my weekly schedule for every hour of the week, and she would approve or deny the schedule. If she thought I was leaving the house too much one day, she would have me remove something like church service, or Christmas service, or an AA meeting, or Celebrate Recovery. She also spent the next two months trying to get Home Depot to release my application because she was convinced, I must have lied about my felonies. She spoke to every store manager and supervisor and even called me while I was working in Lutz one afternoon to tell me to get to her office within the hour. I asked her how I was supposed to do that since I didn't drive. She said, "That's not my problem. Just get here now!"

To get from Lutz to her office in a car takes just about thirty minutes. I didn't have a driver's license and I didn't have anyone scheduled to pick me up at that time. There was no bus I could ride to get there in that time frame. So, I called my wife, and she left work to come get me and take me there. I walked into the probation officer's office, and she said, "Sit down. I have Home Depot Corporate Office on the line with me."

The woman at the corporate office came on the line and said, "Hello, Mr. Seabolt, how are you?"

I said, "Good, is there a problem?"

"We have a request from your probation officer to release your application to her. Do you give us permission to do so?"

I said, "Yes, absolutely."

The woman said to my probation officer, "Officer, if you would like to see Mr. Seabolt's employment application you will have to get a subpoena to do so."

My probation officer was livid. She slammed the phone down and told me to leave her office and quit my job at Home Depot. I am not kidding.

I said, "With all due respect, I can't quit my job. You'll have to go up there and tell them I can't work there."

She replied, "Just get out and go to work." It finally all stopped, and she gave up on the Home Depot thing. She tried her best to get me to react like I would have in the past, but I wasn't the same person any longer, and I was not in charge of myself anymore.

"Or do you not know that your body is a temple of the Holy Spirit within you, whom you have from God? You are not your own, for you were bought with a price. So, glorify God in your body." (1 Cor. 6:19-20 ESV)

Chapter 6
Provision

"And being found in human form, he humbled himself by becoming obedient to the point of death, death on a cross."
(Luke 2:8)

After having the Home Depot job for a while, I began to investigate having my own business because of God's lead to do so. He had me sit in front of a computer until the wee hours of the night to create a website for a "Handyman Business." I didn't even have tools, a license to drive, a vehicle, funds in the bank, a business license, or business sense. I had nothing. Regardless, the business began, and money started coming in from both jobs. After about two years, the Holy Spirit said, "It's time to help Stacey with all the driving." I was thinking, *What? How? I have no license and don't know if I can get a hardship license. I have no vehicle or money to get one, much less pay for the SR-22 insurance I'm going to have to* *have, and the breathalyzer, plus all the fees, fines, and whatever DMV is going to require getting the license.* Yet, it all happened within a month from when He spoke to me.

I worked for a guy who owned a car lot. I was remodeling a property for him at the time. I was looking everywhere else besides his car lot because my old thinking told me not to mix business with pleasure and don't ask for favors from a person I'm working for. About 2 weeks of searching and finally my wife says to me to go to the car lot that my client owns and see if a I can work out a deal with him. My ego then, still needed a little tweaking because when it was time to look, I was looking at all the wrong things. I wanted a nice SUV, a sporty, fancy looking vehicle that spoke to how awesome I am. Yeah, there again, was my old way of thinking. On this car lot, that my client owned there were all those kinds of vehicles and a beige work truck with a rack on it. I asked the car lot owner if I could test drive the SUV. He says, "Don't you think you want to check out the truck?" In my head I'm like *"No"* but I then agreed with him. I had no license yet, so the test drive had to be with my buddy and good friend, Jim who did have a license and was instrumental in helping through this time. We agreed that this was the truck for me. That's where the truck was, God had arranged for me. The hardship license was obtained under certain conditions that I met through His direction and strength. The money for insurance, fines, and fees had all been met and continued to be provided for. I only did one other project for this client after this. Jesus has a plan!

Stacey and I were praying about a trailer to use to help transport all the tools I needed for the handyman business, since riding a bicycle and taking the bus wasn't cutting it any longer. Jim was now working with me from time to time and helping me and the materials to get from job to job when he couldn't work. Jobs were getting bigger, and materials were becoming harder to transport. One Sunday night, we decided to go to a speaker meeting at the Dry Dock in Tarpon Springs, Florida. We pulled into the parking lot and saw a small hauling trailer sitting in an empty parking lot with a sign that said "FREE." Below is an actual picture, with the name and number blotted out of course, but it's the actual sign that was on the trailer.

I looked at Stacey in astonishment and said, "Do you see that?"

She smiled and said, "Yep, you should go check it out!"

I walked over, read the sign, and called the number. The guy answered and said, "Hello."

"I'm standing here at the Dry Dock looking at a trailer and the sign says "Free," what's the deal?"

He replied, "It's yours if you want it. It's good to go. Do you have a way to get it to your house?" I said no and he said, "Okay, I'll tow it there for you. Where do you live?" I told him where I lived and then he said, "You helped me win a bet. My wife said it would probably be there overnight since I was dropping it off so late, but I said I'll give it thirty minutes. You, my friend, called within fifteen minutes of me dropping it off. I barely made it back to the house when you called."

When we think about how God provides for us, we often think of money, job, shelter, food, and protection. What if allowing us to see ourselves as we truly are is provision? I began, many years ago, to think of myself in a certain way and then began to study myself over and over and over. Watching how others reacted to the way I moved, listening to tones of my own voice to understand how others hear what I'm saying and learning what got me the reaction I was looking for. I then adopted those things that worked for whatever situation they were useful for. During these times, as a drug addict, it became more difficult to know who I was or even wanted to be. I had trained myself so well to "shift with the wind" or bend to whatever desire arose in myself, that knowing who I was created to be got buried deep down underneath a lot of lies. Thoughts I kept about others, their reactions, movements, features, got stored away into a mental filing cabinet and then I built mental folders that I believed house specs on everyone. I would pull out these files and practice being these people. I did this to home in on how to be a chameleon given the circumstances. If I had a file labeled "Rugged Man" for example, I would have mental files in them on *How To Stand, How To Form My Facial Expressions, How To Get Angry, How To Be Sorrowful, Aggression,* and *How To Be Sexy, Voice Tones/Talking.* Many other folders as well. It was exhausting.

While in Daytop, a therapeutic community rehabilitation center. Which I touched on earlier. We had an awesome philosophy that we would say every morning at the morning meeting. It was like reciting the "Pledge of Allegiance" in school. It went like this:

> "I am here because there is no refuge finally from myself.
> Until I confront myself in the eyes and hearts of others, I am running.
> Until I suffer them to share my secrets, I have no safety from them.
> Afraid to be known, I can know neither myself nor any other.
> Where else but in our common ground can I find such a mirror?
> Here together, I can at least appear clearly to myself, not as the giant of my dreams, nor the dwarf of my fears, but as a person, part of a whole, with my share in its purpose.
> In this ground, I can take root and grow, not alone anymore, as in death, but alive to myself and to others."

This really resonated with me. I believe it's inspired by the Holy Spirit. The book of James speaks about the man in the mirror, facing the truth about oneself. Not only what you've done but the motives that drive the behaviors. Once I could get down to the truth about myself it was much harder to suppress my feeling and emotions with alcohol and drugs. It wasn't working any longer. I see today this was God working in my life and providing me with tangible memories I could relate to scripture that would come to life and speak about the life Jesus planned for me. These memories would allow me to see how Jesus was prepping me for person He created me to be. Revealing who I am is a daily process. I am more aware of the changes God makes in me today. I see these changes usually after others have taken notice, but I do recognize them first sometimes. It's easy to see when Christ reminds me of who I was in a moment that I don't react the way I used to. He can even remind me of who I don't want to be any longer with a physical memory. Here's a good example.

I asked Stacey if she could take me to my sponsor's house so I could go over my 4th Step with him. This step, for those who are unfamiliar is where the rubber meets the road. This is the step that most people in recovery cringe about just hearing it. This is where you write out and explore your entire life. You dig into your issues and maybe even uncover some you didn't even know you had. You begin to uncover the truth about yourself with God's help. We begin to see ourselves for who we truly were and are. We list out people, places and things, circumstances and situations, memories good and bad, good and bad behaviors, emotional moments, thought life, sexual life, work and home life, harm we caused and harms that were done to us. This is an honest look at ourselves not anyone else. I began to move forward in this step by wanting to bring all the written work I did while in Daytop to my sponsor. Stacey agreed to drive me, so we got into the car and started on our way. She mentioned we should stop to get gas on the way.

We pulled into a gas station, and I noticed someone I had been in jail recently and noticed right away he was on crack. He was searching the floorboards of his car as if he dropped something. His eyes were tweaked wide open, and his facial muscles said it all. I immediately got prideful and wanted to go over and speak to him so he could see that I wasn't like him any longer. That I wasn't using. Like he cared anyways. I had no sympathy, humility, compassion, or love in my heart for him at that moment. When I finally got over to him and yelled out his name and he popped up out of the car, I reached out to shake his hand. When we locked hands, I felt that feeling in my gut like only an addict knows. It went through my body into the very tips of my fingers and toes. I wanted to puke and defecate at the same time. I couldn't believe it. I was confused. I was scared. I didn't understand what was happening. I proceeded into the gas station, paid for gas and got back into the car. Frightened, I looked at Stacey nearly crying, and said, "I'm a drug addict!" The first honest confession I had made. It wasn't that I hadn't confessed that out loud to others before, it was confessing it out loud and meaning it to myself.

God had humbled me in that moment. I had understood what so many had been saying for years. It's the rule for any true alcoholic or drug addict. "Once an alcoholic, always an alcoholic." I believe this is true. I don't believe for one moment that I could ever drink successfully, meaning, once I pick up a drink, I lose the power of choice to put it back down and stay stopped. God has the power to decide whether I drink or not, not me. I am not my own, I have been bought with a price. Jesus has a plan!

My daughter didn't believe me or that any change was real—not the change in me, not the relationship with Jesus, none of it. I asked her if she would put it out there in her own words and this is what she wrote to me for all ya'll.

Hi I'm not sure how long this will be but I kinda wanna just tell you everything I can so you can figure out what you wanna use. I'm gonna try my best to stay linear/make it make sense but yeah any questions let me know. Like I said before, feel free to use anything and it's okay not to use everything. We didn't fully talk about it and i don't know if it's even my place to say but I also wanted to let you know I don't care however you decide to use anything I tell you. Direct quote, summary, paraphrase. It's your book, this is just my story! Love you and super excited to how this journey goes for you.

"So as a child -

For as long as I could remember, I never knew (therefore never understood) your connection to drugs and alcohol. I never put two and two together. Blissfully ignorant I suppose. I don't remember much as a kid but I remember always viewing you as a cool, fun dad for the most part. Looking back, perhaps a little reckless but I had fun lol. On the other side, there were definitely times I was scared of you. I don't really think the fear ever lasted longer than the incident though.

Examples:

there was one night we stayed at Rhonda's (sooooo long ago) after like a bbq thing or something. Of course, you and mom were fighting (AH THATS IT, you and mom fought all the time. That's mostly what I remember about growing up). Anyway, the screaming and yelling woke me up and I was just crying I remember mom picking me up and you went swinging at her with me in her arms. Pure terror for me. Honestly if you want I would fact check this with mom, if she remembers. This is how I remember it, but I was so young I may have it wrong, and I don't wanna be telling you stuff that maybe I don't remember correctly. It's also possible my memory is the only memory, but this is one that has stuck with me.

Another night Nikki was sleeping over at the house and you and mom got into a huge fight and locked you out of the house and you threw a brick through the window of the room we were in. Another memory I would fact check since it was so long ago.

There was another fight between you and mom, and she packed us up in the car to go to grams and you were just yelling and trying to get into the car and banging on the windows and what not. This may have (probably) happened a few times.

Then of course you were in and out of jail. As a kid I really only remember you actually going to jail once when I was in first grade. I don't think you going to jail bothered me though. I remember being really excited to sleep in the car when we drove to the jail to pick you up. I remember there was one day I was really sad though and my teacher asked me what was wrong at recess and I just said, "well my dad's in jail again" and she just looked at me like oh I wasn't prepared for that lol

Just to end the childhood era on a good note here are some good memories I have with you.

I loved having you at practices and sporting events. Cheerleading, soccer, and obviously volleyball are the ones that stick out. You practiced with me a lot and always cheered me on.

We played a lot of pool and I had a lot of fun doing that. I remember you awkwardly bringing up the first time I got my period while we were playing pool lol

I truly truly TRULY thought you were invincible. That's what you always told me. And from seeing you smash beer bottles over your head, light your hand on fire (which you taught me how to do), and countless injuries I believed you couldn't get hurt. I think you believed that too lol but I thought you were super cool for that.

Playing rock band with you (and of course mom) was literally so much fun!!!! All the broken chairs and red faces from laughing so hard. Loved it.

Ok ok so the teenage years/ the time I finally remember realizing alcohol was a problem.

So obviously I also had my own issues in middle school, but I think what stuck out about that time was I didn't trust you. I didn't feel like I could talk to you. I saw you as an angry person. It's hard to say if it was all the alcohol or a mix of that and just the fact, I was a moody teenager starting to dislike my parents. I think this was also the time you had moved out?? I don't remember when that was, but I remember most of the time I wasn't thrilled going to visit you. But then again, I don't think I was thrilled about much. I had a lot of fun skateboarding with you though!

This was also when that incident happened when we were away for a volleyball tournament, and you dumped water on me super freaking early in the morning before my game demanding I get up and practice or run or swim laps in the pool. Not cool, dad. Dying your Mohawk was cool though.

Anyway, so you got arrested in 8th grade (I'm pretty sure) but that's when it clicked. It's really weird cause I wasn't a dumb kid obviously. I knew drinking and driving was wrong. I knew that drinking alcohol made you drunk. But I never remember being around you and thinking "oh he's drunk." I was bummed you went to jail again. I remember going to court and being happy I was missing school. But that's really it. I think I was pretty indifferent towards you.

But then you came back.

Thinking about it now, you sobering up was probably the hardest adjustment for me. All my life I knew you as a "drunk". You could be angry, violent, absent, fun, and adventurous. That was normal for me. And especially at this time I enjoyed you not being around all the time. But then you came back. The best way I remember it was you weren't there for me as a father for so long (it felt) so who the hell do you think you are to start now. I remember being so upset with you when you would tell me to do things (clean my room, normal teenage stuff). But you also yelled a lot, and I didn't like being yelled at. I wasn't mad necessarily mad at you for the past. I was mad because i felt like you needed to earn your spot back in our family, especially as my dad. I was older now, so I understood a lot more. This is kinda sad, I'm sorry. But I was scared for mom. That was my biggest concern when you came back. I hated the way you treated her, and I hated seeing her sad. I never thought she deserved better than you and goodness gracious nothing pissed me off more than y'all deciding to get married. To me you still didn't earn the right to be my father and definitely not her husband. I definitely got caught rolling my eyes at the wedding. But yeah, I think it was also just a huge transition for me to begin with. Starting high school at Gulf which only a couple of my friends went to. I was also starting birth control and that was a disaster lol but yeah you sobering up was rough on me. The only thing that really helped was time and maturity I suppose. There isn't anything that you did that sticks out to me that made me start to be less angry. I just kinda accepted you were back and not going anywhere anytime soon. I do think you finding Jesus and your involvement in the church/the startup of your business did open my eyes a little bit. I saw that you could be considerate and compassionate which I never really saw before.

Not gonna lie, when you first started this new life, I thought it was all bullshit. At least for the first year I always thought "well this isn't gonna last long" or viewed you as a phony, just doing what you think you should be doing to be a good person so other people can see you that way. I thought it was all manipulation. But you stuck with it.

I think it was around senior year that I was on good terms with you. Honestly, I think I was just exhausted. School, work, volleyball, boyfriends, so much going on and I was just too tired. I didn't have the energy to be mad at you all the time. So, I let it go. I stopped trying to poke holes in your actions. I let you do your thing as I did mine. Eventually I began to gain respect for you as I recognized all the work you were doing. By the time I was off to college I was proud of you (not to sound condescending).

Today:

I know I said you getting sober was a hard adjustment on me, but good golly do I now recognize how hard it was for you too. I truly believe you were trying your best and I commend you for that. I'm still so proud of you. You have made so much progress, I never could have imagined this being your life years ago. I'm proud of your ever-growing relationship with god, the work you put in to constantly improve your relationship with mom, everything you've had to overcome to get your business where it is now, your sobriety and your persistence. You haven't given up. I admire that. You've worked to earn my trust, respect, and love and I'm thankful for that. I'm thankful to have you around now. I know I can depend on you. And I full heartedly believe mom is in good hands now, so thank you for being there for her as well. I also never thought I would be a mom, so this never even crossed my mind but I'm so thankful you get to be a part of Ella's life and she gets to grow up with a grandpa. It's a relationship I never thought I'd see but I'm very glad it's there.

My advice: (to those reading this)

Give grace. People CAN change if you're willing to change your view of them as well. Let go of the past and learn to forgive. You only have control of yourself. You can't control the actions

> of others, but you can control how you respond to them. It's okay to be emotional. Be angry. Be hurt. Be sad. But move forward.
>
> I love you dad! This is definitely a lot longer than I thought it would be and I'm sorry if it's sucks to read. But good luck!!! "

WOW!!! I cry every time I read that letter. I cry because of who I no longer am and what I neglected. I am reminded that I was hurting my wife and hurting my daughter. I cry because of the gratitude I now have come to know. I am truly blessed by God. I know that having Stacey and Danielle still in my life, and the fact that they talk to me, live life with me, and love me is not usual for a story like this. I still don't believe it most days.

Here my daughter is talking about showing a little grace that incorporates forgiveness. You don't get one without the other, and which comes first is a harder question then, "Which comes first, the chicken or the egg?" Jesus' work at the cross is just this. The truth we search for is found in Him. He is the grace of God unto salvation. His purpose in coming here was for the forgiveness of sins. Adam brought death to many, and Jesus brought us life. This is provision.

The provisions Jesus has made for us to be with our Father is mind boggling. The way He continues to provide for me and our family is mind boggling to me still today. These short stories and moments are just clips of how Jesus has put things together and I will continue to write about it in other books. The ways He has orchestrated my walk in recovery rooms, work life, and church is no different today. I'm the same man in church, at home or in the grocery store. Jesus deserves all honor and glory. Not some, ALL! It's not me who does anything but trust in Him who created me.

Chapter 7
Hope

*"You are my hiding place and my shield,
I hope in your word"
(Psalm 119:114 ESV)*

Most will say, "I can't forgive myself for these things I've done!" Like I said earlier, you're right. See, it's like this, God created everything when there was nothing. After He created the first man and woman, they disobeyed some directions or commands, rules if you will. How and why, that took place is in the mind of God, and we can debate whether Adam loved Eve more than he wanted to be obedient or that Adam was a coward and did not perform his priestly duties. Either way, it went the way it was ordained to go by God to move His plan forward. Out of that little debacle we gained sin in the world, the world that God created and said was good. We now have disease, horrific tragedy, painstaking trouble, overwhelming desires, and hatred toward our own Creator. So much so that we, some of us, will try everything we can to prove He is nonexistent. Most of us will deny His existence and live out the rest of our days as the god of our own lives.

God will instruct, guide, and teach us His very own convictions in the simplest ways. Throughout history, He has allowed us to learn what our human nature is designed to be and do. He has shown us that there are desires, wants, and needs that can only be satisfied by Him, in us and through us. The Lord will bring people to Himself to use as His voice piece. They are called prophets that do not claim to be Him. There will be wars fought in and on His behalf and for His glory. Many will die horrible deaths, children will be slain and slaughtered, and women raped, abused, mistreated, and killed. These things violate people's consciences and cause shame and guilt to manifest and become like a weight in their hearts and minds until something can be done to remove it. These things will only take place if God allows them to happen and has ordained them to be written into existence. These are hard truths to hear I know. Since these things happen regularly, I wouldn't allow myself to believe in God much less Jesus. I couldn't understand how a loving God would allow such things to take place in a world He loved and said was good.

If you read the Old Testament, you're going to see animal sacrifices everywhere for everything. Read Hebrews and you'll see the nature of what animal sacrifices were meant to be and do for the human being. You'll learn that animal sacrifice was necessary for the forgiveness of sins, even for the priests, but those sacrifices were lacking in a way that could not atone for a complete blotting out of human sins, your sins, mine, theirs, and all sins to come. There is a consequence for sin, and although it may seem silly to say, we can see the consequences, usually very visibly and quickly. There are weighty internal consequences that are experienced and no matter how hard you try they will never be removed. Jesus has a plan. Living life will teach us there's nothing powerful enough on earth, no human power, no enhanced enlightenment, no pill, no psychiatrist or psychologist, no program or steps, no meetings or self-help, no meditation, no letters of grief, or no works we learn in Bible studies or groups that will remove the internal experienced consequences of sin. They only pacify a sinner, which brings us to why we need a savior.

> *Psalm 14:3 "They have all turned aside; together they have become corrupt; there is no one who does good, not even one." (ESV)*

When sin or wrongdoing according to Gods laws and commands started from the beginning, we see this statement is Psalms 14 to be true. None of us is left exempt. We are all sinners according to God. We can't get it right. Only He knows the right thing to do and when we become born again by believing in Jesus and answering the call on our lives to come to Jesus, then in His mighty name, we learn and are led by the Holy Spirit to do the right thing. Not always will we be obedient to the teacher. This is where grace and mercy collide.

> *"The wages of sin is death, but the free gift of God is eternal life in Christ Jesus our Lord." according to Romans 6:23 (ESV)*

Here's where we see Jesus, and this is why we are called sinners. This is why we need a savior. Because the blood of goats and bulls would only be good for the flesh and not last. To solve the sin problem there needed to be death. God, in the Old Testament, handed out laws to be adhered to and there was to be animal sacrifices to atone for the sins of man who broke the law. These animals that were used for sacrifices had to be the best of the best. They were without blemishes. These were the perfect animals. When the priests or people who would kill the animals in the way God described to, they would offer these sacrifices to God in ritualistic ways. In all cases the blood was important and sprinkled over things and people in some cases.

Sacrifices were like payments for a debt. When someone owes you money back because you lent them money, and they don't pay you, it's frustrating correct? What if they only pay a little bit back and don't complete the payment process? You just aren't going to be quite satisfied until you receive payment in full. This is what God is asking for. For us to pay our debt for breaking His laws. We needed to learn that our payments were not enough to satisfy our debt, that we weren't able to do this on our own, satisfy this debt to God. Here's the question. What is the payment you believe is required to satisfy the debt you own, to earn your forgiveness? What would you need to do or repay to satisfy that requirement. If you don't believe you need to repay or do anything, then maybe you aren't in need of forgiveness as you see it. Not everyone needs a doctor.

Now, these offerings/sacrifices would only remove the sins of the people and the priests for one year, they weren't satisfying the debt requirement in full. Every year they would need to atone for their sins in this way. There was still a problem as you can see. Why weren't their sins removed completely? Which is a great question and one I have asked myself. I learned by reading in Hebrews that these sacrifices did not remove the internal weight of sin in a human being. "What is this weight?", you might ask. Another great question. It's the weight we all suffer with because of sin. It's condemnation. When we wrong someone or ourselves most of us feel something that doesn't feel very good. These feelings are internal and cannot be removed by animal blood or sacrifice. This the Bible says, are the feelings of condemnation. The feelings that burden us daily, long after sin has taken place. Condemnation is built out of shame and guilt. These two internal consequences are heavier than anything you'll ever experience, and nothing can make them stop haunting a person except the payment that grants complete forgiveness for sin.

Jesus came as the ultimate sacrifice to be killed or sacrificed, and his blood became the one thing that will atone, remove the weight, and grant complete forgiveness of sins. This God would have to do Himself, again because none of us are good enough to be the perfect sacrifice. We all have blemishes. He sent His own son to be like us, to be killed for us, for you and for me so our sins could be forgiven. Once and for all time. See, it's not your job to forgive yourself. Jesus was sent here to be the atonement to grant you your forgiveness. You can't earn it yourself, you and me, we aren't a good enough payment. If you don't believe Jesus is God, please read this and I pray the Holy Spirit opens your eyes, ears and hearts to receive it:

"[1] In the beginning was the Word, and the Word was with God, and the Word was God. [2] He was with God in the beginning. [3] Through him all things were made; without him nothing was made that has been made. [4] In him was life, and that life was the light of all mankind. [5] The light shines in the darkness, and the darkness has not overcome[a] **it**.*

"[14] The Word became flesh and made his dwelling among us. We have seen his glory, the glory of the one and only Son, who came

from the Father, full of grace and truth." John 1:1-5, 14 (ESV)

My sin brought condemnation, which led to death and brought me to repentance. Repentance is like prerequisites to faith in Jesus. It's only through true repentance, surrendering to the fact that I can't change myself and I am nothing, brought about by the Holy Spirit did I receive grace. That is forgiveness. It's not that I did anything, but that God did everything. Repentance is not only being sorry about something, but also remorse, change of heart, change of behavior, it's knowledge of good and evil, it's knowing truth and seeing the lies, it's thinking differently, it's a different way of life.

If you don't know the story of what Jesus endured—how He was beaten, had his skin torn from His body, and much more very graphic details that bring me to tears to even think about, before He was killed. He did this while being sinless and blameless to buy my forgiveness, your forgiveness, for all the things we've done and the person I was, so I could have peace once again with God like it was supposed to from the beginning—then I pray He quickens you, speaks to you, and saves you!

Stacey and I share our testimony together and separately. We are involved in Recovery because it's where He wants us to be. Knowing today that "recovery" is not just for alcoholics, drug and sex addicts, it's for everyone. The steps are designed to show the everyday person how to find God, how to walk out their faith, how to pour out all the "old wine" and get rid of the "old wine skin" to make room for the "new wine skin" because it needs to be strong enough to hold all the new wine! This all comes from the Bible where Bill and Bob, founders of AA, got the steps.

> *[33] And they said to him, "The disciples of John fast often and offer prayers, and so do the disciples of the Pharisees, but yours eat and drink." [34] And Jesus said to them, "Can you make wedding guests fast while the bridegroom is with them? [35] The days will come when the bridegroom is taken away from them, and then they will fast in those days." [36] He also told them a parable: "No one tears a piece from a new garment and puts it on an old garment. If he does, he will tear the new, and the piece from the new will not match the old. [37] And no one puts new wine*

> *into old wineskins. If he does, the new wine will burst the skins and it will be spilled, and the skins will be destroyed. ^{38} But new wine must be put into fresh wineskins. ^{39} And no one after drinking old wine desires new, for he says, 'The old is good.' Luke 5:33-39 (ESV)*

If you remember, I have a middle brother named Mike. On June 19, 2023, Jesus took away a thirty-year crack addiction, and he was saved at fifty-seven years old. Today, he knows Jesus and wants everyone to know it, just like I do. I cried for days after he called and told me over the phone. I got to see him while on a trip to New Jersey and he looked different. We are now working on our relationship as brothers, and it's just so awesome! We get to walk out our salvation together and that's more precious than I understand right now. Jesus loves showing off, and I love being a spectator. Jesus has a plan!

It hasn't ended yet with the way God answers our prayers, directs our steps, and helps us to walk out His plan for our lives. I don't believe He will ever stop. To this day, we walk with Christ as our leader. He's the head of our home, He's the boss of our jobs, He's the judge in our life, He's the author and finisher of our faith, He's my creator, He's your creator, and He's the Alpha and Omega, baby! I'm a nobody, yelling to tell everybody, all about the God who saved my soul. These are paraphrased lyrics from a Casting Crowns song called, "Nobody."

Lord Jesus, you are amazing and worthy to be praised in every way we can. Thank you, Lord, for saving me. Thank you for changing me and thank you for loving me.

God bless ya'll. I hope you cry out to Him because He will answer. Lord, speak to these hearts, open their eyes and their ears, remove their hearts of stone, and give them a heart of flesh, remove the veil. Help them to take up their mat and walk. You alone are the Holy One. You alone are the Lord. You alone are the most high Jesus Christ our Lord! Continue your work, Father. Help us to be obedient to your call on our lives and move us where You will. I pray in Jesus' mighty name, the name above all names, Amen!

> *"And I will sow her for myself in the land. And I will have mercy on No Mercy, and I will say to Not My People, 'You are my people'; and he shall say, 'You are my God."(Hosea 2:23)*

One last thing. Love is no longer a mountain in my life. Jesus moves mountains! I received love one day and now I know love, I give love, and love lives in me, and I pray He lives in you. Thanks for letting me share!

Printed in the USA
CPSIA information can be obtained
at www.ICGtesting.com
LVHW050536181124
796659LV00007B/120